To obtain your [E...]
use the coupo[n ...]

USA and CANADA

Enclose 50¢ in coin,
check or money order

BRITISH ISLES

Enclose 20p in
check or postal order

ALL OTHER COUNTRIES

Enclose equivalent of 50¢
(half a US dollar) in check
or money order or in postage
stamps valid in your own
country

Mail to:

Berlitz Hebrew Record

P.O. Box 741
Midtown Station,
New York, N.Y. 10018

Berlitz Hebrew Record

Pembroke House,
Campsbourne Road,
London N.8. 7PT.

Either one of the addresses above

To: BERLITZ Hebrew Record   17

....

....

Please send me your pronunciation record.

name: ....

address: ....

....

zip or postal code: ....

city: ....

country: ....

I enclose.............................
for postage and handling

☐ check

☐ money order

☐ coin (USA and
   Canada only)

☐ postage stamps

This offer is subject to local import restrictions and may be cancelled without notice
when present stocks of the record are depleted.

Berlitz Travellers Series

Phrase Books:

Danish, Dutch, European (14 languages), Finnish, French, German. Greek, Hebrew, Italian, Japanese, Norwegian, Polish, Portuguese, Russian, Serbo-Croatian, Spanish, Latin American Spanish, Swahili, Swedish, Turkish

Bilingual Pocket Dictionaries:

Danish, Dutch, Finnish, French, German, Italian, Norwegian, Spanish, Swedish

LP Records:

Danish, Dutch, Finnish, French, German, Italian, Norwegian, Portuguese, Spanish, Latin American Spanish, Swedish

Cassettes:

Danish, Dutch, Finnish, French, German, Hebrew, Italian, Norwegian, Portuguese, Russian, Spanish, Latin American Spanish, Swedish

Cartridges:

French, German, Italian, Spanish, Latin American Spanish

Berlitz phrase books, dictionaries and audio materials are also available for travellers speaking Danish, Dutch, Finnish, French, German, Italian, Japanese, Norwegian, Serbo-Croatian, Spanish and Swedish. For complete information, write to:

Editions Berlitz S.A.
3, avenue des Jordils
1006 Lausanne, Switzerland

HEBREW

FOR TRAVELLERS

By the Staff of Editions Berlitz

Editions Berlitz S.A., Lausanne, Switzerland

Library of Congress Catalog Card Number: 73-2274

First Printing 1974.
Second Printing 1974.
Printed in Belgium

Berlitz Trademark Reg. U.S. Patent Office
and other countries—Marca Registrada

Editions Berlitz S.A.
3, avenue des Jordils
1006 Lausanne, Switzerland

Preface

You are about to visit Israel. Our aim is to give you a new and more practical type of phrase book to help you on your trip.

Hebrew for Travellers provides:

* all the phrases and supplementary vocabulary you will need on your trip

* a wide variety of tourist and travel facts, tips and useful information

* a complete phonetic transcription, showing you the pronunciation of all the words and phrases listed

* an audio-aid in the form of a pronunciation record (a cassette of over 300 key phrases is also available)

* special sections showing the replies your listener might give to you—just hand him the book and let him point at the appropriate phrase. This is especially practical in certain difficult situations (doctor, car mechanic, etc.). It makes direct, quick and sure communication possible

* a logical system of presentation so that you can find the right phrase for the immediate situation

* quick reference through colour coding. The major features of the contents are on the back cover; a complete index is given inside.

These are just a few of the practical advantages. In addition, the book will prove a valuable introduction to life in Israel.

There is a comprehensive section on Eating Out, giving translations and explanations for practically anything one would find on a menu in Israel; there is a complete Shopping Guide that will enable you to obtain virtually anything you want. Trouble with the car? Turn to the mechanic's manual with its dual-language instructions. Feeling ill? Our medical section provides the most rapid communication possible between you and the doctor.

As an added and special feature, we have included six pages of useful phrases in Arabic.

To make the most of *Hebrew for Travellers*, we suggest that you start with the "Guide to Pronunciation". Then go on to "Some Basic Expressions". This not only gives you a minimum vocabulary; it helps you to pronounce the language. The entire section has been recorded by native speakers. Send for the record (see page 1).

We are particularly grateful to Mr. Mario Zielinski for his help in the preparation of this book, and to Mr. Moshe Rosen who devised the phonetic transcription. We also wish to thank the Israel Government Tourist Office and the staff of Keter Publishing House, Jerusalem, for their assistance.

We shall be very pleased to receive any comments, criticisms and suggestions that you think may help us in preparing future editions.

Thank you. Have a good trip.

Guide to pronunciation

The alphabet

Here are the characters which comprise the Hebrew alphabet; capital letters do not exist. The left-hand column shows the handwritten characters, the middle column printed characters, and with the right-hand column you can pronounce their names in Hebrew. Five characters (צ,פ,נ,מ,כ) take a different form when appearing at the end of a word, as shown.

אָ	א	alef
ג	ב	bet
ג	ב	vet
ג	ג	gimel
ף	ד	dalet
ה	ה	he
ו	ו	vav
ז	ז	zain
ח	ח	het
ט	ט	tet
י	י	yod
כ	כ	kaf
ך	ך	khaf
ל	ל	lamed
מ,ם	מ,ם	mem
נ,ן	נ,ן	nun
ס	ס	samekh
ע	ע	ain
פ	פ	pe
פ,ף	פ,ף	fe
צ,ץ	צ,ץ	tzadi
ק	ק	kof
ר	ר	resh
ש	ש	shin
ש	ש	sin
ת	ת	tav

PRONUNCIATION

This, of course, is not enough to pronounce Hebrew. We're offering you a helping hand by providing "imitated pronunciation" throughout this book. This and the following section are intended to make you familiar with the transliteration we devised and to help you get used to the sounds of the language. As a minimum vocabulary for your trip, we have selected a number of basic words and phrases under the title "Some Basic Expressions" (pages 11–16). That selection serves another purpose. Recorded by native speakers of Hebrew, it forms the script for our pronunciation record (see page 1).

An outline of the sounds of Hebrew

The traditional Hebrew script is composed of consonants only and is written from right to left. A system of vowel signs (dots and lines with the characters), used mainly in poetry, in liturgical writing and in texts for beginners—including this phrase book—ensures proper pronunciation.

A transliteration is a representation of the sounds of the language in our alphabet, as opposed to the traditional Hebrew alphabet. It can be read quite easily once a few rules have been mastered. In these transliterations, letters shown in bold print should be read with more stress (louder) than the others. All vowels must be pronounced distinctly. Apart from **ey** and **ay**, there are no diphthongs in the transliteration.

If you follow carefully the indications supplied below, you will have no difficulty in reading the transliterations in such a way as to make yourself understood. In addition, listening to the native speakers on the record and constant practice will help you to improve your accent. (This book also contains the Hebrew script. If, despite your efforts, your listener does not seem to understand you, then show him or her the book and indicate what you want to say).

Letter	Approximate pronunciation	Example	
א	agrees with vowel sign (see below) and is pronounced accordingly **a**, **e**, **i**, **o** or **u**	אָמַר	amar
		אֶשְׁכּוֹלִית	eshkolit
		אִשָּׁה	isha
		אוֹר	or
		אוּלְפָּן	ulpan
בּ	like **b** in boy	בּוּל	bul
ב	like **v** in very	בָּבֶל	Bavel
ג	like **g** in gold	גָּמָל	gamal
ד	like **d** in day	דָּג	dag
ה	like **h** in hail	הֶגֶה	hege
ו	1) like **v** in very	וֶרֶד	vered
	2) may also serve as a vowel and is then pronounced **o** or **u**	אוּלָם	ulam
		אוֹלָר	olar
ז	like **z** in zeal	זֶמֶר	zemer
ח	like **ch** in the Scottish loch (symbol used ḥ)	חַיָּט	ḥayat
ט	like **t** in tip	טַיָּס	tayas
י	1) like **y** in yard	יֶלֶד	yeled
	2) may also serve as a vowel and is then pronounced **i**	שִׁירָה	shira
כ	like **k** in kite	כָּתַב	katav
כ / ך	like **ch** in the Scottish loch, (a "soft" כ); symbol used **kh**	מִכְתָּב	mikhtav
		פָּרִיךְ	parikh
ל	like **l** in let	לָשׁוֹן	lashon
מ / ם	like **m** in come	מָלוֹן	malon
		מַיִם	mayim
נ / ן	like **n** in not	נַעֲרָה	naara
		שָׁעוֹן	shaon
ס	like **s** in sit	סוֹחֵר	soḥer

ע	agrees with vowel sign and is pronounced accordingly **a**, **e**, **i**, **o** or **u**	עָמַד	amad
		עֶזְרָה	ezra
		עִתּוֹן	iton
		עוֹרֵךְ־דִּין	orekh di
		עוּגָּה	uga
פ	like **p** in **p**ot	פַּרְדֵּס	pardes
פ / ף	(a "soft" פ) like **f** in **f**it	קָפֶה	kafe
		עוֹף	of
צ / ץ	like **ts** in hi**ts**	צֶמֶר	tzemer
		נַעַץ	naatz
ק	like **k** in **k**ite	בֹּקֶר	boker
ר	a gargling **r** sound, like in the French word **r**i**r**e	תַּפְרִיט	tafrit
שׁ	like **sh** in **sh**oulder	שֶׁמֶשׁ	shemesh
שׂ	like **s** in **s**it	שְׂמִיכָה	semikha
ת	like **t** in **t**ip	תּוֹדָה	toda

Note: The letters א, ו, י can also function as vowels depending on the vowel sign:

א	like **a**, **e**, **o**, **i** or **u**
ו	**o** or **u**
י	like **i**

Vowel signs

Vowel signs and dots occur mostly under the letter; sometimes inside or over it. They are pronounced **after** the letter that carries the sign, e.g.: פָּשׁוּט pashut.

The system of vowel signs is as follows:

אַ/אֲ/אָ	pronounced as the vowel sound in but (symbol used a)	סָפַר	sapar
		אֲגַם	agam

אֶ/אֱ/אֵ	pronounced as **e** in n**e**t	אֶרֶץ	eretz
		אֱמֶת	emet
		שֵׂכֶל	sekhel
אִ	pronounced as **ee** (symbol used i) in m**ee**t	רִבָּה	riba
		גִּיטָרָה	gitara
אָ/אוֹ/אֹ	pronounced as **o** in p**o**t	אֹהֶל	ohel
		שׁוֹטֵר	shoter
		אֳנִיָּה	oniya
אֻ/אוּ	pronounced as **oo** (symbol used u) in b**oo**t	לַחוּת	lahut
		שֻׁלְחָן	shulhan
אְ	pronounced as a half-vowel; something like **e** in happ**e**ning	לְחַיִּים	lehayim

Some basic expressions

Yes.	כֵּן.	ken ✗
No.	לֹא.	lo ✗
Please.	בְּבַקָּשָׁה.	bevakasha ✗
Thank you.	תּוֹדָה.	toda ✗
Thank you very much.	תּוֹדָה רַבָּה.	toda raba ✗
That's all right.	בְּבַקָּשָׁה.	bevakasha ✗

Greetings

Good morning.	בֹּקֶר טוֹב.	boker tov
Good afternoon.	שָׁלוֹם.	shalom
Good evening.	עֶרֶב טוֹב.	erev tov
Good night.	לַיְלָה טוֹב.	layla tov
Good-bye.	שָׁלוֹם.	shalom
See you later.	לְהִתְרָאוֹת.	lehitraot
This is Mr. . . .	נָא לְהַכִּיר אֶת אָדוֹן...	na lehakir et adon . . .
This is Mrs. . . .	נָא לְהַכִּיר אֶת גְּבֶרֶת...	na lehakir et geveret . . .
This is Miss . . .	נָא לְהַכִּיר אֶת גְּבֶרֶת...	na lehakir et geveret . . .

Note:
As pointed out in the grammar section, verbs in Hebrew change their endings according to whether a man or a woman is speaking. They also change if the person addressed is a man or a woman. In this section, the phrases said to a **man** are marked with **one** asterisk (*); those said to a **woman** are marked with **two** asterisks (**). Phrases not marked do not change.

I'm very pleased to meet you.	נָעִים מְאֹד.	naim meod
How are you?	מַה שְׁלוֹמֵךְ?**	ma shelomekh**
Very well, thank you.	טוֹב, תּוֹדָה.	tov, toda
And you?	וְאַתָּה?*	veata
Fine.	טוֹב.	tov
Excuse me.	סְלַח לִי.*	selah li

Questions

Where?	אֵיפֹה?	eyfo
Where is . . . ?	אֵיפֹה...?	eyfo
Where are . . . ?	אֵיפֹה...?	eyfo
When?	מָתַי?	matay
What?	מַה?	ma
How?	אֵיךְ?	ekh
How much?	כַּמָּה?	kama
How many?	כַּמָּה?	kama
Who?	מִי?	mi
Why?	לָמָה?	lama
Which?	אֵיזֶה?	eyze
What do you call this?	אֵיךְ זֶה נִקְרָא?	ekh ze nikra
What do you call that?	אֵיךְ זֶה נִקְרָא?	ekh ze nikra
What does this mean?	מַה פֵּרוּשׁ הַדָּבָר הַזֶּה?	ma perush hadavar haze
What does that mean?	מַה פֵּרוּשׁ הַדָּבָר הַזֶּה?	ma perush hadavar haze

Do you speak . . . ?

Do you speak English?	אַתָּה מְדַבֵּר אַנְגְּלִית?*	ata medaber anglit*
Do you speak German?	אַתָּה מְדַבֵּר גֶּרְמָנִית?*	ata medaber germanit*
Do you speak French?	אַתָּה מְדַבֵּר צָרְפָתִית?*	ata medaber tzarfatit*
Do you speak Spanish?	אַתָּה מְדַבֵּר סְפָרָדִית?*	ata medaber sefaradit*
Do you speak Italian?	אַתָּה מְדַבֵּר אִיטַלְקִית?*	ata medaber italkit*
Could you speak more slowly, please?	אַתָּה יָכוֹל לְדַבֵּר יוֹתֵר לְאַט, בְּבַקָּשָׁה?*	ata yakhol ledaber yoter leat, bevakasha*
Please point to the phrase in the book.	תַּרְאֶה לִי אֶת הַמִּשְׁפָּט בַּסֵּפֶר, בְּבַקָּשָׁה.*	tare li et hamishpat basefer, bevakasha*
Just a minute. I'll see if I can find it in this book.	רֶגַע בְּבַקָּשָׁה. אֲחַפֵּשׂ בַּסֵּפֶר.	rega bevakasha. ahapes basefer
I understand.	אֲנִי מְבִינָה.	ani mevina
I don't understand.	אֲנִי לֹא מֵבִין.	ani lo mevin

Can . . . ?

Can I have . . . ?	אֲנִי יָכוֹל לְקַבֵּל . . .?	ani yakhol lekabel
Can we have . . . ?	אֲנַחְנוּ יְכוֹלִים לְקַבֵּל . . .?	anahnu yekholim lekabel
Can you show me . . . ?	אַתָּה יָכוֹל לְהַרְאוֹת לִי . . .?*	ata yakhol leharot li*
Can you tell me . . . ?	אַתְּ יְכוֹלָה לְהַגִּיד לִי . . .?**	at yekhola lehagid li**
Can you help me, please?	אַתְּ יְכוֹלָה לַעֲזוֹר לִי, בְּבַקָּשָׁה?**	at yekhola laazor li, bevakasha**

Wanting

I'd like . . .	הָיִיתִי רוֹצָה . . .	hayiti rotza
We'd like . . .	הָיִינוּ רוֹצִים . . .	hayinu rotzim
Please give me . . .	תֵּן לִי ; בְּבַקָשָׁה . . .*	ten li, bevakasha*
Give it to me, please.	תְּנִי לִי אוֹתוֹ, בְּבַקָשָׁה.**	teni li oto, bevakasha**
Please bring me . . .	תָּבִיאִי לִי, בְּבַקָשָׁה . . .**	tavii li, bevakasha**
Bring it to me, please.	תָּבִיא לִי אוֹתוֹ, בְּבַקָשָׁה.*	tavi li oto, bevakasha*
I'm hungry.	אֲנִי רְעֵבָה.	ani reeva
I'm thirsty.	אֲנִי צָמֵא.	ani tzame
I'm tired.	אֲנִי עֲיֵפָה.	ani ayefa
I'm lost.	נֶאֱבַדְתִּי.	neevadeti
It's important.	זֶה חָשׁוּב.	ze hashuv
It's urgent.	זֶה דָחוּף.	ze dahuf
Hurry up!	תִּזְדָרְזִי!**	tizdarzi**

It is/There is . . .

It is/It's . . .	זֶה . . .	ze
Is it . . . ?	הַאִם זֶה . . . ?	haim ze
It isn't . . .	זֶה לֹא . . .	ze lo
There is/There are . . .	יֵשׁ . .	yesh
Is there/Are there . . . ?	הַאִם יֵשׁ . . . ?	haim yesh
There isn't/There aren't . . .	אֵין . . .	en
There isn't any/ There aren't any.	אֵין.	en

A few common words

big/small	גָּדוֹל / קָטָן	gadol/katan
quick/slow	מָהִיר / אִטִּי	mahir/iti
early/late	מֻקְדָּם / מְאֻחָר	mukdam/meuhar
cheap/expensive	זוֹל / יָקָר	zol/yakar
near/far	קָרוֹב / רָחוֹק	karov/rahok
hot/cold	חַם / קַר	ham/kar
full/empty	מָלֵא / רֵיק	male/rek
easy/difficult	קַל / קָשֶׁה	kal/kashe
heavy/light	כָּבֵד / קַל	kaved/kal
open/shut	פָּתוּחַ / סָגוּר	patuah/sagur
right/wrong	נָכוֹן / לֹא נָכוֹן	nakhon/lo nakhon
old/new	יָשָׁן / חָדָשׁ	yashan/hadash
old/young	זָקֵן / צָעִיר	zaken/tzair
beautiful/ugly	יָפֶה / מְכוֹעָר	yafe/mekhoar
good/bad	טוֹב / לֹא טוֹב	tov/lo tov
better/worse	יוֹתֵר טוֹב / יוֹתֵר גָּרוּעַ	yoter tov/yoter garua

A few prepositions and some more useful words

at	בְּ–	be
on	עַל	al
in	בְּ–	be
to	לְ–	le
from	מ–	mi
inside	בְּתוֹךְ	betokh
outside	בַּחוּץ	bahutz
up	לְמַעְלָה	lemala
down	לְמַטָּה	lemata

before	לִפְנֵי	lifney
after	אַחֲרֵי	aharey
with	עִם	im
without	בְּלִי	beli
through	דֶּרֶךְ	derekh
towards	בְּכִוּוּן	bekhivun
until	עַד	ad
during	מֶשֶׁךְ	meshekh
and	וְ–	ve
or	אוֹ	o
not	לֹא	lo
nothing	כְּלוּם	kelum
none	אַף אֶחָד	af ehad
very	מְאֹד	meod
also	גַּם	gam
soon	בְּקָרוֹב	bekarov
perhaps	אוּלַי	ulay
here	כָּאן	kan
there	שָׁם	sham
now	עַכְשָׁו	akhshav
then	אָז	az

A very basic grammar

General

Modern Hebrew as it is now spoken in Israel is a direct offshoot from classical Hebrew, the language of the Bible. At the turn of the century, the spoken language was revived and adapted to suit contemporary ways of living. Its vocabulary was extended and adapted, partly by the absorption of a number of foreign words and even phrases.

Today, there is no field of activity where Hebrew does not have its own terminology, from science right down to the most mundane daily use. The structure of the language has remained the same. Basically, it is concise, to the point and meaningful. It is a Semitic language and therefore differs structurally from English and European concepts of language. It is written from right to left.

Articles

The definite article (**the**) in Hebrew is הַ (ha) for both masculine and feminine genders in the singular and in the plural. It pre-ceeds—beware—the noun as well as the adjective. E.g.:

מָלוֹן	malon	hotel
טוֹב	tov	good
הַמָּלוֹן	hamalon	the hotel
הַמָּלוֹן הַטּוֹב	hamalon hatov	the good hotel

There is no indefinite article (a/an). To give indefinite meaning, the definite article is simply omitted.

Nouns

There are two genders: masculine and feminine. Nouns ending in **e** are generally masculine, as well as all nouns with typically masculine bearing. As a general rule, nouns ending in **a**, with the accent on the last syllable, are feminine; so are the names of towns and countries and all nouns denoting female properties and forms. E.g.:

Masculine			**Feminine**		
מוֹרֶה	more	teacher	מִטָּה	mita	bed
חָתוּל	ḥatul	cat	מַלְכָּה	malka	queen
אַבָּא	aba	father	סְפָרַד	Sefarad	Spain

Basically, the plurals are formed by adding the ending **-im** to masculine words and **-ot** to feminine words. However, exceptions and irregular endings are so numerous that it is difficult to give any rule of thumb. A few examples:

regular:

חָבֵר	ḥaver	boy friend	חֲבֵרִים	ḥaverim	boy friends
חֲבֵרָה	ḥavera	girl friend	חֲבֵרוֹת	ḥaverot	girl friends

irregular:

(masc.) שֻׁלְחָן	shulḥan	table	שֻׁלְחָנוֹת	shulḥanot	tables
(fem.) שָׁנָה	shana	year	שָׁנִים	shanim	years

Adjectives

Adjectives do not come before the noun, as in English, but after it. They agree with the noun in gender and number. E.g.:

צֶבַע חוּם	tzeva ḥum	brown colour
מִזְוָדוֹת חוּמוֹת	mizvadot ḥumot	brown suitcases

Possessive adjectives agree with the possessor, not with the thing possessed. They also come after the noun.

Masculine			Feminine		
my	שֶׁלִּי	sheli	my	שֶׁלִּי	sheli
your	שֶׁלְּךָ	shelkha	your	שֶׁלָּךְ	shelakh
his	שֶׁלּוֹ	shelo	her	שֶׁלָּה	shela
our	שֶׁלָּנוּ	shelanu	our	שֶׁלָּנוּ	shelanu
your	שֶׁלָּכֶם	shelakhem	your	שֶׁלָּכֶן	**shelakhen**
their	שֶׁלָּהֶם	shelahem	their	שֶׁלָּהֶן	shelahen

Verbs

One particularity of Hebrew verbs is that they change their endings not only according to the subject (I, you, he, etc.), but also according to whether that subject is a man or a woman (or the subject noun is masculine or feminine). To give you an idea, here is the conjugation in past, present and future of the verb "to write":

	Past tense wrote	Present tense write	Future tense will write
I	katavti	kotev	ekhtov
you (masc.)	katavta	kotev	tikhtov
you (fem.)	katavt	kotevet	tikhtevi
he	katav	kotev	ikhtov
she	katva	kotevet	tikhtov
we	katavnu	kotevim	nikhtov
you (masc. pl.)	ketavtem	kotevim	tikhtevu
you (fem. pl.)	ketavten	kotevot	tikhtevu
they (masc. pl.)	katvu	kotevim	ikhtevu
they (fem. pl.)	katvu	kotevot	ikhtevu

Moreover, the verb forms also change according to whether a man or a woman is being spoken to. You will find some examples of this in "Some basic expressions". In the rest of this phrase book all verbs are given in the masculine form unless the content is specifically feminine (as in the beauty parlour).

The negative is formed by the word **lo** (לֹא), meaning both "no" and "not".

	Present	Past	Future
affirmative	אֲנִי אוֹכֵל (ani okhel) I eat	אֲנִי אָכַלְתִּי (ani akhalti) I ate	אֲנִי אֹכַל (ani okhal) I shall eat
negative	אֲנִי לֹא אוֹכֵל (ani lo okhel) I don't eat	אֲנִי לֹא אָכַלְתִּי (ani lo akhalti) I didn't eat	אֲנִי לֹא אֹכַל (ani lo okhal) I won't eat

GRAMMAR

Personal pronouns

Subject			Direct object		
I	אֲנִי	ani	me	אוֹתִי	oti
you (masc.)	אַתָּה	ata	you (masc.)	אוֹתְךָ	otkha
you (fem.)	אַתְּ	at	you (fem.)	אוֹתָךְ	otakh
he	הוּא	hu	him	אוֹתוֹ	oto
she	הִיא	hi	her	אוֹתָהּ	ota
we	אֲנַחְנוּ	anahnu	us	אוֹתָנוּ	otanu
you	אַתֶּם	atem	you	אֶתְכֶם	etkhem
they	הֵם	hem	them	אוֹתָם	otam

Arrival

You've arrived. Whether you've come by ship or plane, you'll have to go through passport and customs formalities. (For car/border control, see page 145.)

There's certain to be somebody around who speaks English. That's why we're making this a brief section. What you really want is to be off to your hotel in the shortest possible time. Here are the stages for a speedy departure.

Passport control

In these days of the jumbo jet, you may well be waved through passport control with a smile. Otherwise:

Here's my passport.	הִנֵּה הַדַּרְכּוֹן.	hine hadarkon
I'll be staying . . .	אֶשָּׁאֵר...	eshaer
a few days	כַּמָּה יָמִים	kama yamim
a week	שָׁבוּעַ	shavua
two weeks	שְׁבוּעַיִם	shevuayim
a month	חוֹדֶשׁ	ḥodesh
I don't know yet.	עוֹד אֵינֶנִּי יוֹדֵעַ.	od eyneni yodea
I'm here on holidays.	אֲנִי כָּאן בְּחֻפְשָׁה.	ani kan beḥufsha
I'm here on business.	אֲנִי כָּאן לְרֶגֶל עֲסָקִים.	ani kan leregel asakim
I'm just passing through.	אֲנִי רַק בְּמַעֲבָר.	ani rak bemaavar

If things become difficult:

I'm sorry, I don't understand. Is there anyone here who speaks English?	אֲנִי מִצְטַעֵר, אֲנִי לֹא מֵבִין. יֶשׁ כָּאן מִישֶׁהוּ שֶׁמְּדַבֵּר אַנְגְּלִית?	ani mitztaer, ani lo mevin. yesh kan mishehu shemdaber anglit

Customs

Believe it or not, the customs officials are just as eager to wave you through as you are to go.

The chart below shows you what you can bring in duty free*.

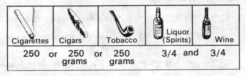

Cigarettes	Cigars	Tobacco	Liquor (Spirits)	Wine
250 or	250 grams or	250 grams	3/4 and	3/4

Israel has adopted what is becoming a customs clearance practice everywhere. Only some arriving travellers are spot-checked. After collecting your luggage, you have a choice: follow the green arrow if you have nothing to declare. Or, leave via a doorway marked with a red arrow if you have items to declare (in excess of those allowed).

| GOODS to declare | מובין להצהרה | אין מובין להצהרה | NOTHING to declare |

I've nothing to declare.	אֵין לִי מַה לְהַצְהִיר.	en li ma lehatzhir
I've . . .	יֵשׁ לִי...	yesh li
a carton of cigarettes	קַרְטוֹן סִיגָרִיּוֹת	karton sigariyot
a bottle of whisky	בַּקְבּוּק וִיסְקִי	bakbuk whisky
a bottle of wine	בַּקְבּוּק יַיִן	bakbuk yayin
Must I pay on this?	צָרִיךְ לְשַׁלֵּם בִּשְׁבִיל זֶה?	tzarikh leshalem bishvil ze

*All allowances subject to change without notice and measurements approximate. Although customs officers hardly ever quibble about the difference between a litre bottle and a quart bottle, they do have the right to be literal if they choose.

How much?	כַּמָה?	kama
It's for my personal use/ It's not new.	זֶה לְשָׁמוּשׁ אִישִׁי / זֶה לֹא חָדָשׁ.	ze leshimush ishi/ ze lo hadash

---

Possible answers

אַתָה צָרִיךְ לְשַׁלֵם מֶכֶס עַל זֶה.	You'll have to pay duty on this.
שַׁלֵם בַּמִשְׂרָד, שָׁם.	Please pay at the office over there.
יֵשׁ לְךָ עוֹד מִטְעָן?	Have you any more luggage?

Baggage—Porters

Porter!	סַבָּל!	sabal
Can you help me with my luggage?	תּוּכַל לַעֲזוֹר לִי עִם הַמִזְוָדוֹת?	tukhal laazor li im hamizvadot
That's mine.	זֶה שֶׁלִי.	ze sheli
The big/small/blue/ brown/plaid one.	זֶה הַגָדוֹל / הַקָטָן / הַכָּחוֹל / הַחוּם / הַמְשֻׁבָּץ.	ze hagadol/hakatan/ hakahol/hahum/ hameshubatz
There's one piece missing.	חָסֵר אֶחָד.	haser ehad
Take these bags to the ...	קַח אֶת הַמִזְוָדוֹת ...	kah et hamizvadot
taxi	לַמוֹנִית	lamonit
bus	לָאוֹטוֹבּוּס	laotobus
luggage lockers	לְתָאֵי הַמִטְעָן	letaey hamitan
Get me a taxi, please.	תַּשִׂיג לִי מוֹנִית, בְּבַקָשָׁה.	tasig li monit, bevakasha
Where do I catch the bus/taxi for the air terminal?	אֵיפֹה הָאוֹטוֹבּוּס / הַמוֹנִית לִשְׂדֵה־הַתְעוּפָה?	eyfo haotobus/ hamonit lisde-hateufa
How much is that?	כַּמָה זֶה עוֹלֶה?	kama ze ole

Note: The normal rate is 1 pound per bag. Have some small change ready.

Changing money

You'll find a bank at most airports. If it's closed, don't worry. You'll be able to change money at your hotel.

Full details about money and exchange are given on pages 134–136.

I want to change some . . .	אֲנִי רוֹצֶה לְהַחֲלִיף כַּמָה...	ani rotze lehaḥlif kama
traveller's cheques	הַמְחָאוֹת נוֹסְעִים	hamḥaot nosim
dollars	דוֹלָרִים	dolarim
pounds	לִירוֹת שְׁטֶרְלִינְג	lirot sterling
Where's the nearest bank?	אֵיפֹה הַבַּנְק הַקָּרוֹב בְּיוֹתֵר?	eyfo habank hakarov beyoter
What's the exchange rate?	מַהוּ שַׁעַר הַחֲלִיפִין?	mahu shaar haḥalifin

ARRIVAL

Directions

How do I get to . . . ?	אֵיךְ מַגִּיעִים לְ...?	ekh magiim le
Is there a bus into town?	יֵשׁ אוֹטוֹבּוּס הָעִירָה?	yesh otobus haira
Where can I get a taxi?	אֵיפֹה מוֹצְאִים מוֹנִית?	eyfo motzim monit
Where can I rent a car?	אֵיפֹה אֶפְשָׁר לִשְׂכּוֹר מְכוֹנִית?	eyfo efshar liskor mekhonit

Hotel reservations

Obviously it's safest to book in advance if you can. But if you haven't done so?

Many terminals have a hotel reservation service or tourist information office. You're sure to find somebody there who speaks English.

FOR NUMBERS, see page 175

Car rental

Again it's best to make arrangements in advance whenever possible. There are car rental firms at most airports and terminals. It's highly likely that someone there will speak English. But if nobody does, try one of the following . . .

I'd like . . .	. . . הָיִיתִי רוֹצֶה לִשְׂכּוֹר	hayiti rotze liskor
a small car	מְכוֹנִית קְטַנָּה	mekhonit ketana
a large car	מְכוֹנִית גְּדוֹלָה	mekhonit gedola
a sports car	מְכוֹנִית סְפּוֹרט	mekhonit sport
for a day/four days	לְיוֹם אֶחָד / לְאַרְבָּעָה יָמִים	leyom eḥad/learbaa yamim
a week/two weeks	לְשָׁבוּעַ / לִשְׁבוּעַיִם	leshavua/lishvuayim
What's the charge per day?	כַּמָּה זֶה עוֹלֶה לְיוֹם?	kama ze ole leyom
What's the charge per week?	כַּמָּה זֶה עוֹלֶה לְשָׁבוּעַ?	kama ze ole leshavua
Does that include mileage?	כּוֹלֵל קִילוֹמֶטרַגְ'?	kolel kilometrage
Is petrol (gasoline) included?	כּוֹלֵל דֶּלֶק?	kolel delek
Does that include full insurance?	כּוֹלֵל בִּטּוּחַ מַקִּיף?	kolel bituaḥ makif
What's the deposit?	מַה הַפִּקָּדוֹן?	ma hapikadon
I have a credit card.	יֵשׁ לִי כַּרְטִיס אַשְׁרַאי.	yesh li kartis ashray

Note: In Israel, any current driving licence is normally sufficient, but it must be accompanied by an authorized translation if it's not in English or French. An International Driving Permit may come in handy.

| Here's my driving licence. | הִנֵּה רִשְׁיוֹן הַנְּהִיגָה שֶׁלִּי. | hine rishyon hanehiga sheli |

FOR SIGHTSEEING, see page 73

ARRIVAL

Taxi

All taxis have meters. It's usually best to ask the approximate fare beforehand. For some trips (e.g. airport to town) there may be a fixed fare. This will be posted at the airport. Taxi drivers don't expect to be tipped.

Many taxi companies operate a *sherut* service in and between the main cities. Some of them operate on the sabbath. The word *sherut* means service; seats are sold on an individual basis with up to seven persons sharing the same cab. In the towns, the *sherut* follow the main bus routes. Fares are 10% to 30% higher than bus fares.

Where can I get a taxi?	אֵיפֹה אֶפְשָׁר לְהַשִּׂיג מוֹנִית?	eyfo efshar lehasig monit
Get me a taxi, please.	תַּשִּׂיג לִי מוֹנִית, בְּבַקָּשָׁה.	tasig li monit, bevakasha
What's the fare to . . . ?	כַּמָּה עוֹלָה הַנְּסִיעָה לְ . . . ?	kama ola hanesia le
How far is it to . . . ?	מַה הַמֶּרְחָק לְ . . . ?	ma hamerhak le
Take me to . . .	קַח אוֹתִי . . .	kah oti
this address/the town centre/the . . . hotel	לַכְּתוֹבֶת הַזֹּאת / לְמֶרְכַּז הָעִיר / לָמָלוֹן . . .	laktovet hazot/lemerkaz hair/lamalon
Turn left at the next corner.	פְּנֵה שְׂמֹאלָה בַּפִּנָּה הַבָּאָה.	pene smola bapina habaa
Go straight ahead.	תַּמְשִׁיךְ יָשָׁר.	tamshikh yashar
Stop here, please.	עֲצֹר כָּאן, בְּבַקָּשָׁה.	atzor kan, bevakasha
I'm in a hurry.	אֲנִי מְמַהֵר.	ani memaher
There's no hurry.	אַל תְּמַהֵר.	al temaher
Could you drive more slowly?	אַתָּה יָכוֹל לִנְסוֹעַ יוֹתֵר לְאַט?	ata yakhol linsoa yoter leat

Hotel— Other accommodation

Early reservation (and confirmation) is essential in most major tourist centres during the high season. You may have to pay a supplementary charge on Jewish high holydays.

Hotels in Israel are classified thus:

* * * * * Luxury class
* * * * First class
* * * Middle class
* * Tourist class
* Simple tourist class

Only hotels classified in one of these categories are recommended for tourists.

HOTEL

Accommodation in kibutzim

Many of Israel's *kibutzim* (collective agricultural settlements) run their own guest houses to allow outsiders to get an idea of their unique social structure. They're just as clean and comfortable as any hotel and offer complete privacy. Usually country-style food is served. Although there's no obligation to participate in communal activities, the administration may be able to arrange for you to spend your time in the fields if you're interested. Such working holidays in *kibutzim* can also be arranged in advance.

Youth hostels

These offer dormitory accommodation. Blankets are provided and sheets may be hired for a small additional charge. Most of them serve meals and all offer kitchen facilities. Group reservations must be made in advance.

In this section, we're mainly concerned with the smaller and middle-grade hotels. You'll have no language difficulties in the luxury and first-class hotels where most of the staff have been trained to speak English.

In the next few pages we consider your basic requirements, step by step, from arrival to departure. You need not read through it all; just turn to the situation that applies.

Checking in—Reception

My name is . . .	שְׁמִי . . .	shemi
I have a reservation.	הִזְמַנְתִּי מָקוֹם.	hizmanti makom
We've reserved two rooms, a single and a double.	הִזְמַנּוּ שְׁנֵי חֲדָרִים, אֶחָד לְיָחִיד וְאֶחָד זוּגִי.	hizmannu sheney hadarim, ehad leyahid veehad zugi
I wrote to you last month. Here's the confirmation.	כָּתַבְתִּי לָכֶם בַּחוֹדֶשׁ שֶׁעָבַר. הִנֵּה הָאִשּׁוּר.	katavti lakhem bahodesh sheavar. hine haishur
I'd like . . .	הָיִיתִי רוֹצֶה . . .	hayiti rotze
a single room	חֶדֶר לְיָחִיד	heder leyahid
a double room	חֶדֶר זוּגִי	heder zugi
two single rooms	שְׁנֵי חֲדָרִים לְיָחִיד	sheney hadarim leyahid
a room with twin beds	חֶדֶר עִם שְׁתֵּי מִטּוֹת	heder im shetey mitot
a room with a bath	חֶדֶר עִם אַמְבַּטְיָה	heder im ambatya
a room with a shower	חֶדֶר עִם מִקְלַחַת	heder im miklahat
a room with a balcony	חֶדֶר עִם מִרְפֶּסֶת	heder im mirpeset
a room with a view	חֶדֶר עִם נוֹף	heder im nof
a suite	מַעֲרֶכֶת־חֲדָרִים	maarekhet hadarim
We'd like a room . . .	אֲנַחְנוּ רוֹצִים חֶדֶר . . .	anahnu rotzim heder
in the front	בְּחָזִית	behazit
at the back	אֲחוֹרִי	ahori
facing the sea	מוּל הַיָּם	mul hayam
facing the park	מוּל הַגַּן	mul hagan

It must be quiet.	הָעִקָּר חֶדֶר שָׁקֵט.	haikar ḥeder shaket
Is there . . . ?	הַאִם יֵשׁ . . . ?	haim yesh
air conditioning	מִזּוּג אַוִּיר	mizug avir
heating	חִמּוּם	ḥimum
a radio (television)	רַדְיוֹ (טֶלֶוִיזְיָה)	radio (televizia)
in the room	בַּחֶדֶר	baḥeder
a laundry	מִכְבָּסָה	mikhbasa
room service	הַגָּשָׁה לַחֶדֶר	hagasha laḥeder
hot water	מַיִם חַמִּים	mayim ḥamim
running water	מַיִם זוֹרְמִים	mayim zormim
a private toilet	נוֹחִיּוּת בְּנִפְרָד	noḥiyut benifrad

How much ?

What's the price . . . ?	כַּמָּה עוֹלֶה הַחֶדֶר . . . ?	kama ole haḥeder
per night	לְלַיְלָה	lelayla
per week	לְשָׁבוּעַ	leshavua
for bed and breakfast	לִינָה וַאֲרוּחַת־בּוֹקֶר	lina vearuḥat boker
excluding meals	בְּלִי אֲרוּחוֹת	beli aruḥot
for full board	כּוֹלֵל אֲרוּחוֹת	kolel aruḥot
Does that include meals/service ?	הַמְּחִיר כּוֹלֵל אֲרוּחוֹת וְשֵׁרוּתִים?	hamehir kolel aruḥot vesherutim
Is there any reduction for children ?	יֵשׁ הֲנָחָה לִילָדִים?	yesh hanaḥa liyladim
Do you charge for the baby ?	מְשַׁלְּמִים בִּשְׁבִיל הַתִּינוֹק?	meshalmim bishvil hatinok
That's too expensive.	יוֹתֵר מִדַּי יָקָר.	yoter miday yakar
Haven't you anything cheaper ?	יֵשׁ מַשֶּׁהוּ יוֹתֵר זוֹל?	yesh mashehu yoter zol

FOR NUMBERS, see page 175

HOTEL

How long?

We'll be staying . . .	נִשָׁאֵר . . .	nishaer
overnight only	רַק לַיְלָה אֶחָד	rak layla eḥad
a few days	יָמִים אֲחָדִים	yamim aḥadim
a week	שָׁבוּעַ	shavua
don't know yet.	עוֹד לֹא בָּטוּחַ	od lo batuaḥ

Decision

May I see the room?	אֶפְשָׁר לִרְאוֹת אֶת הַחֶדֶר?	efshar lirot et haḥeder
No, I don't like it.	הוּא לֹא מוֹצֵא חֵן בְּעֵינַי.	hu lo motze ḥen beeynay
It's too . . .	הוּא יוֹתֵר מִדַי . . .	hu yoter miday
cold/hot	קַר / חַם	kar/ḥam
dark/small	חָשׁוּךְ / קָטָן	ḥashukh/katan
noisy	רוֹעֵשׁ	roesh
I asked for a room with a bath.	בִּקַשְׁתִּי חֶדֶר עִם אַמְבַּטְיָה.	bikashti ḥeder im ambatya
Have you anything . . . ?	יֵשׁ לָכֶם מַשֶׁהוּ . . . ?	yesh lakhem mashehu
better/bigger	יוֹתֵר טוֹב / יוֹתֵר גָדוֹל	yoter tov/yoter gadol
cheaper/quieter	יוֹתֵר זוֹל / יוֹתֵר שָׁקֵט	yoter zol/yoter shaket
That's fine. I'll take it.	בְּסֵדֶר גָמוּר. אֶקַח אוֹתוֹ.	beseder gamur. ekaḥ oto.

HOTEL

Bills

These are usually submitted weekly or when you're leaving if you stay less than a week. For children, if no separate room is required for them, there's a reduction of 50% up to the age of 6 and 30% for 6 to 12 year olds.

Tipping

A service charge (15–20%) is normally included in the bill, but you can ask:

Is service included?	כּוֹלֵל שֵׁרוּת?	kolel sherut

Tipping is moderate in Israel. Half a pound will do for the man who carries your bags to your room. Leave 10 pounds per week for the chambermaid. Tip your waiter and the porter at the time you leave.

Registration

On arrival at a hotel or boarding house you'll be asked to fill in a registration form (*tofes*). It asks your name, home address, passport number and further destination. It's almost certain to carry an English translation. If it doesn't, ask the desk clerk:

What does this mean?	מַה כָּתוּב כָּאן?	ma katuv kan

The desk clerk will probably ask you for your passport. He may want to keep it for a while, even overnight. Don't worry— you'll get it back. The desk clerk may want to ask you the following questions:

אֲנִי יָכוֹל לִרְאוֹת אֶת הַדַּרְכּוֹן?	May I see your passport?
נָא לְמַלֵּא אֶת טוֹפֶס הַהַרְשָׁמָה.	Would you mind filling in this registration form?
נָא לַחְתּוֹם.	Sign here, please.
כַּמָה זְמָן תִּשָּׁאֵר?	How long will you be staying?

What's my room number?	מַה מִסְפָּר הַחֶדֶר שֶׁלִי?	ma mispar haheder sheli
Will you have our bags sent up?	הַאִם תַּעֲלוּ אֶת הַמִּזְוָדוֹת לַחֶדֶר?	haim taalu et hamizvadot laheder

Service, please

Now that you're safely installed, meet some more of the hotel staff.

the chambermaid	חַדְרָנִית	hadranit
the manager	מְנַהֵל	menahel
the telephone operator	מֶרְכָּזָנִית	merkazanit
the valet	חַדְרָן	hadran

Call the members of the staff *Adoni* (sir) or *Geveret* (miss) when calling for service.

General requirements

Please ask the chambermaid to come up.	אֲבַקֵשׁ אֶת הַחַדְרָנִית.	avakesh et hahadranit
Who is it?	מִי שָׁם?	mi sham
Just a minute.	רֶגַע אֶחָד.	rega ehad
Come in!	יָבוֹא!	yavo
Is there a bath on this floor?	יֵשׁ אַמְבַּטְיָה בַּקוֹמָה הַזֹאת?	yesh ambatya bakoma hazot
Please send up . . .	אֲבַקֵשׁ לִשְׁלֹחַ לַחֶדֶר...	avakesh lishloah laheder
two coffees/a sandwich	שְׁנֵי קָפֶה / סֶנְדְבִיץ'	sheney kafe/sandwich
two gin and tonics	שְׁנֵי ג'ִין וְטוֹנִיק	sheney gin ve tonik
Can we have breakfast in our room?	אֶפְשָׁר לְקַבֵּל אֲרוּחַת-בֹּקֶר בַּחֶדֶר?	efshar lekabel aruhat boker baheder
I'd like to leave these in your safe.	אֲנִי רוֹצֶה לִשְׁמֹר אֶת זֶה בַּכַּסֶפֶת.	ani rotze lishmor et ze bakasefet
Can you find me a babysitter?	תּוּכַל לִמְצֹא לִי "בֵּיבִּי־סִיטֶר"?	tukhal limtzo li baby sitter
May I have a/an/ some . . . ?	אֶפְשָׁר לְקַבֵּל...?	efshar lekabel
ashtray	מַאֲפֵרָה	maafera
bath towel	מַגֶבֶת	magevet

HOTEL SERVICE

extra blanket	שְׂמִיכָה נוֹסֶפֶת	semikha nosefet
envelopes	מַעֲטָפוֹת	maatafot
(more) hangers	(עוֹד) קוֹלָבִים	(od) kolavim
hot-water bottle	בַּקְבּוּק חַם	bakbuk ḥam
ice	קֶרַח	keraḥ
needle and thread	חוּט וָמַחַט	ḥut vamaḥat
extra pillow	כַּר נוֹסָף	kar nosaf
reading lamp	מְנוֹרַת לַיְלָה	menorat layla
soap	סַבּוֹן	sabon
writing paper	נְיָר כְּתִיבָה	neyar ketiva
Where's the . . . ?	אֵיפֹה...?	eyfo
bathroom	חֲדַר הָאַמְבַּטְיָה	ḥadar haambatya
beauty parlour	מְכוֹן הַיוֹפִי	mekhon hayofi
cocktail lounge	הַבַּר	habar
dining room	חֲדַר־הָאֹכֶל	ḥadar haokhel
hairdresser's	הַמִּסְפָּרָה	hamispara
television room	חֲדַר הַטֶּלֶוִיזְיָה	ḥadar hatelevizia
toilet	נוֹחִיּוּת	noḥiyut
restaurant	מִסְעָדָה	misada

HOTEL SERVICE

Breakfast

An Israeli breakfast consists of dairy products such as sour milk, yoghurt, cheese, butter, eggs and vegetables. However, most hotels are able to provide a continental or American breakfast. So ask:

I'll have a/an/ some . . .	אֶקַּח לִי...	ekaḥ li . . .
cereal	דַּיְסָה	daysa
hot/cold	חַמָּה / קָרָה	ḥama/kara
eggs	בֵּיצִים	beytzim
boiled egg	בֵּיצָה מְבֻשֶּׁלֶת	beytza mevushelet
soft/medium/hard	רַכָּה / בֵּינוֹנִי / קָשָׁה	raka/beynoni/kasha
fried	בֵּיצָה מְטֻגֶּנֶת	beytza metugenet
scrambled	בֵּיצָה מְקֻשְׁקֶשֶׁת	beytza mekushkeshet

fruit juice	מִיץ פֵּרוֹת	mitz peyrot
grapefruit/orange	אֶשְׁכּוֹלִיּוֹת / תַּפּוּזִים	eshkoliyot/tapuzim
pineapple/tomato	אַנָּנָס / עַגְבָנִיּוֹת	ananas/agvaniyot
omelet	חֲבִיתָה	havita
sausages	נַקְנִיקִיּוֹת	naknikiyot
May I have some . . . ?	אֶפְשָׁר לְקַבֵּל...?	efshar lekabel . . .
hot/cold milk	חָלָב חַם / קַר	halav ham/kar
cream/sugar	שַׁמֶּנֶת / סוּכָּר	shamenet/sukar
salt/pepper	מֶלַח / פִּלְפֵּל	melah/pilpel
coffee/tea	קָפֶה / תֵה	kafe/te
chocolate	קָקָאוֹ	kakao
lemon/honey	לִימוֹן / דְבָשׁ	limon/devash
Could you bring me a . . . ?	תָבִיא לִי, בְּבַקָשָׁה ...?	tavi li bevakasha
plate	צַלַּחַת	tzalahat
glass	כּוֹס	kos
cup	סֵפֶל	sefel
knife	סַכִּין	sakin
fork	מַזְלֵג	mazleg
spoon	כַּף	kaf

Note: You'll find a great many other dishes listed in our guide "Eating Out" (pages 38–64). This should be consulted for your lunch and dinner menus.

HOTEL SERVICE

Difficulties

The . . . doesn't work.	הַ ... מְקֻלְקָל.	ha . . . mekulkal
air conditioner	מַזְגָן אַוִיר	mazgan avir
fan	מְאַוְרֵר	meavrer
light	חַשְׁמַל	hashmal
tap	בֶּרֶז	berez
toilet	נוֹחִיּוּת	nohiyut

HOTEL SERVICE

The wash basin is blocked.	הַכִּיּוֹר סָתוּם.	hakiyor satum
The window is jammed.	הַחַלּוֹן נִתְפַּס.	hahalon nitpas
The blind is stuck.	הַתְּרִיס נִתְפַּס.	hatris nitpas
These aren't my shoes.	נַעֲלַיִם אֵלֶּה לֹא שֶׁלִּי.	naalayim ele lo sheli
This isn't my laundry.	כְּבִיסָה זֹאת לֹא שֶׁלִּי.	kevisa zot lo sheli
There's no hot water.	אֵין מַיִם חַמִּים.	en mayim hamim
I've lost my watch.	אָבַד לִי הַשָּׁעוֹן.	avad li hashaon
I've left my key in my room.	הִשְׁאַרְתִּי אֶת הַמַּפְתֵּחַ בַּחֶדֶר.	hisharti et hamafteah baheder
The . . . is broken.	הַ . . . מְקֻלְקָל.	ha . . . mekulkal
bulb	נוּרָה	nura
lamp	מְנוֹרָה	menora
plug	תֶּקַע	teka
shutter/window shade	תְּרִיס / וִילוֹן	tris/vilon
switch	מַפְסִיק	mafsik
Can you get it fixed?	תּוּכַל לְתַקֵּן אֶת זֹאת?	tukhal letaken et zot

Telephone—Mail—Callers

Can you get me Tel-Aviv 123456?	תַשִּׂיגִי לִי, בְּבַקָּשָׁה, תֵּל־אָבִיב 123456.	tasigi li, bevakasha, Tel-Aviv 123456
Has anyone telephoned me?	הָיְתָה שִׂיחָה בִּשְׁבִילִי?	hayta siha bishvili
Is there any mail for me?	הִגִּיעַ דֹּאַר בִּשְׁבִילִי?	higia doar bishvili
Have you any stamps?	יֵשׁ לְךָ בּוּלִים?	yesh lekha bulim
Would you mail this for me, please?	שְׁלַח אֶת זֶה בַּדֹּאַר, בְּבַקָּשָׁה.	shelah et ze badoar, bevakasha
Are there any messages for me?	נִתְקַבְּלָה הוֹדָעָה בִּשְׁבִילִי?	nitkabla hodaa bishvili

FOR POST OFFICE, see page 137

Checking out

May I have my bill, please? Room 398.	אֶפְשָׁר לְקַבֵּל אֶת הַחֶשְׁבּוֹן? חֶדֶר 398.	efshar lekabel et hakheshbon? kheder 398
I'm leaving early tomorrow.	אֲנִי עוֹזֵב מָחָר הַשְׁכֵּם בַּבֹּקֶר.	ani ozev makhar hashkem baboker
Please have my bill ready.	תָּכִין, בְּבַקָשָׁה, אֶת הַחֶשְׁבּוֹן.	takhin, bevakasha, et hakheshbon
We'll be checking out around noon.	אֲנַחְנוּ עוֹזְבִים בַּצָּהֳרַיִם.	anakhnu ozevim batzohorayim
I must leave at once.	עָלַי לַעֲזוֹב מִיָּד.	alay laazov miyad
Does this include service?	זֶה כּוֹלֵל שֵׁרוּת?	ze kolel sherut
Is everything included?	הַכֹּל כָּלוּל בַּחֶשְׁבּוֹן?	hakol kalul bakheshbon
You've made a mistake in this bill, I think.	נִדְמֶה לִי שֶׁיֵּשׁ טָעוּת בַּחֶשְׁבּוֹן.	nidme li sheyesh taut bakheshbon
Can you get us a taxi?	תַּזְמִין לָנוּ מוֹנִית, בְּבַקָשָׁה.	tazmin lanu monit, bevakasha
When's the next. . . to Haifa?	מָתַי יוֹצֵא. . . לְחֵיפָה?	matay yotze . . . le Haifa
bus/train/ car	הָאוֹטוֹבּוּס / הָרַכֶּבֶת / הַמְכוֹנִית	haotobus/harakevet/ hamkhonit
Would you send someone to bring down our baggage?	שְׁלַח מִישֶׁהוּ, בְּבַקָשָׁה, לְהוֹרִיד אֶת הַמִּזְוָדוֹת.	shelakh mishehu, bevakasha, lehorid et hamizvadot
We're in a great hurry.	אֲנַחְנוּ מְמַהֲרִים מְאֹד.	anakhnu memaharim meod
Here's the forwarding address. You have my home address.	הִנֵּה הַכְּתוֹבֶת שֶׁלִּי לְהַעֲבָרַת דֹּאַר; וְהִנֵּה הַכְּתוֹבֶת שֶׁלִּי בַּבַּיִת.	hine haktovet sheli lehaavarat doar; vehine haktovet sheli babayit
It's been a very enjoyable stay.	נֶהֱנֵיתִי מְאֹד כָּאן.	nehneyti meod kan

Eating out

There are many different kinds of eating and drinking places in Israel.

בֵּית קָפֶה
(bet kafe)

Coffee house. The coffee house is a favourite Israeli haunt. Your drinks will generally be cheaper at the counter. Food isn't normally served, except for cakes (or cookies) and sandwiches. There may be several kinds of coffee available.

מִילְק שֵׁיק
(milk shake)

Milk shake bar. Milk shakes and ice cream are served.

מִסְעָדָה
(misada)

A restaurant. These are classified as follows according to the standard of cuisine and service:

 3 forks in a circle—outstanding
(equivalent of four stars)

 3 forks—excellent
(equivalent of three stars)

 2 forks—very good
(equivalent of two stars)

 1 fork—good
(equivalent of one star)

סְטֵיקִיָּה
(steakiya)

Steak house. This is a snack shop with a few tables where light dishes such as *humus*, *tehina* and salads can be had. Grilled steaks, often served in *pita*, are also served.

סֶנְדְוִיצְ׳יָה (sandwichiya)	Sandwich shop where all sorts of sandwiches are available. The number of Israel's sandwich shops is rapidly increasing.
פָלָפֶל (falafel)	Small stand or shop where you can buy Israel's most popular snack. *Falafel* is the equivalent of the American hot dog or the British fish and chips. It's basically small balls of ground chick peas, fried and served in *pita* (oriental bread).
קְיוֹסק (kiosk)	Stands serving fresh fruit juice, cold beverages and *gazoz*. This is fruit syrup with carbonated water.

In this section we're primarily concerned with restaurants—and with lunch and dinner. We assume that you've already had breakfast at your hotel (for a breakfast menu, see page 34). Big restaurants display a menu in the window.

You'll find many specialized restaurants. There's a choice of French, Italian, Oriental, Hungarian, Romanian and other places, so there's something for every taste.

To get a table in a well-known restaurant, telephone in advance.

Note: Most restaurants close on Saturdays (*shabbat*), except Arab restaurants.

Meal times

אֲרוּחַת צָהֳרַיִם (aruhat tzohorayim)	Lunch. Can be served at any time in fact, but is mostly from noon to 2 p.m.
אֲרוּחַת עֶרֶב (aruhat erev)	Dinner, starting around 6 p.m. and continuing till late.

EATING OUT

What is kosher?

The word *kosher* (כָּשֵׁר) means clean or fit according to Jewish dietary laws. Most of the problems you'll have with kosher meals will come from the basic prohibition against eating dairy and meat products together. These problems may be partially solved by using vegetal butter (margarine) instead of animal butter. Nevertheless, you'll be surprised when you see how the Israeli cooks have found ways to substitute products to elude these problems. At kosher establishments you'll not get cheese or milk with or after a meat dish.

According to kosher laws, only animals which have split hooves and chew their cud are edible. These are the two principal requirements. Animals that don't fulfill both conditions are forbidden. Pigs, for instance, have split hooves but don't chew their cud. The camel chews its cud but doesn't have split hooves and is therefore forbidden, too. As to fish, all edible seafood must have scales and fins. Shellfish, whales and porpoises aren't edible under this criterion.

Most of the restaurants you'll find in Israel are ruled by kosher laws; however, there are a few Arab restaurants able to provide you with non-kosher specialties such as shellfish, meat dishes cooked in butter, cheese or sauces made of dairy products.

Don't let rumours about kosher restrictions discourage you. You'll probably not even notice that you're having your meals according to kosher legislation. You may even be agreeably surprised by the variety of dishes available.

Hungry?

Can you recommend a good and inexpensive restaurant?	תוּכַל לְהַמְלִיץ עַל מִסְעָדָה טוֹבָה וְלֹא יְקָרָה?	tukhal lehamlitz al misada tova velo yekara
I'd like to reserve a table for four, for eight o'clock tonight.	אֲנִי רוֹצֶה לְהַזְמִין שׁוּלְחָן לְאַרְבָּעָה, לְשָׁעָה שְׁמוֹנֶה הָעֶרֶב.	ani rotze lehazmin shulhan learbaa, leshaa shemone haerev

Asking and ordering

Good evening. I'd like a table for three.	עֶרֶב טוֹב; אֲבַקֵשׁ שׁוּלְחָן לִשְׁלוֹשָׁה.	erev tov; avakesh shulhan lishlosha
Could we have a . . . ?	אֶפְשָׁר לְקַבֵּל . . . ?	efshar lekabel
table in the corner	שׁוּלְחָן בַּפִּנָּה	shulhan bapina
table by the window	לְיַד הַחַלּוֹן	leyad hahalon
table on the terrace	עַל הַמִּרְפֶּסֶת	al hamirpeset
quiet table somewhere	בְּמָקוֹם שָׁקֵט	bemakom shaket
Where are the toilets?	אֵיפֹה הַנּוֹחִיּוּת?	eyfo hanohiyut
What's the price of the fixed menu?	כַּמָּה עוֹלָה אֲרוּחָה אֲחִידָה?	kama ola aruha ahida
Is service included?	כּוֹלֵל שֵׁרוּת?	kolel sherut
Could we have a(n) . . . please?	אֶפְשָׁר לְקַבֵּל . . . ?	efshar lekabel
ashtray	מַאֲפֵרָה	maafera
bottle of . . .	בַּקְבּוּק . . .	bakbuk
glass	כּוֹס	kos
glass of water	כּוֹס מַיִם	kos mayim
knife	סַכִּין	sakin
napkin	מַפִּית	mapit
plate	צַלַּחַת	tzalahat
spoon	כַּף	kaf
toothpick	קִסְמִים לְשִׁנַּיִם	kismim leshinayim

EATING OUT

FOR COMPLAINTS, see page 55

I'd like a/an/some. . .	תֵּן לִי, בְּבַקָּשָׁה . . .	ten li, bevakasha
beer	בִּירָה	bira
bread	לֶחֶם	lehem
butter	חֶמְאָה	hema
cheese	גְּבִינָה	gevina
chips (french fries)	צְ׳יפְּס	chips
coffee	קָפֶה	kafe
fish	דָּג	dag
fruit	פֵּירוֹת	peyrot
ice-cream	גְּלִידָה	gelida
lemon	לִימוֹן	limon
lettuce	חַסָּה	hasa
meat	בָּשָׂר	basar
milk	חָלָב	halav
mustard	חַרְדָּל	hardal
olive oil	שֶׁמֶן זַיִת	shemen zayit
pepper	פִּלְפֵּל	pilpel
potatoes	תַּפּוּחֵי־אֲדָמָה	tapuhey-adama
poultry	עוֹף	of
rice	אוֹרֶז	orez
rolls	לַחְמָנִיּוֹת	lahmaniyot
salad	סָלָט	salat
salt	מֶלַח	melah
sandwich	סֶנְדְּבִיץ׳	sandwich
soup	מָרָק	marak
spaghetti	אִטְרִיּוֹת	itriyot
sugar	סוּכָּר	sukar
tea	תֵּה	te
vegetables	יְרָקוֹת	yerakot
vinegar	חוֹמֶץ	hometz
water	מַיִם	mayim
wine	יַיִן	yayin

What's on the menu ?

Our menu has been presented according to courses. Under each heading you'll find an alphabetical list of dishes in Hebrew with their English equivalents. This list—which includes everyday and special dishes—will enable you to make the most of an Israeli menu.

Here's our guide to good eating and drinking. Turn to the course you want to start with.

EATING OUT

Obviously, you're not going to go through every course on the menu. If you've had enough, say:

Nothing more, thanks.　　　זֶה הַכֹּל, תּוֹדָה.　　ze hakol, toda

Israeli food is very tasty and offers a wide range of specialities according to the origins of restaurant owners. Hot and spicy oriental dishes are as frequently found as Central European dishes. French cooking is popular, too. The only thing you'll have to keep in mind is the kosher law.

Appetizers—Starters

Shellfish isn't kosher. However, you'll find it in some Arab
restaurants in the coastal area, e.g. in Akko, Haifa, Jaffa and
other places.

Israeli people prefer salads as appetizers, but restaurant
and cooking have become such an important activity in
Israel that all requests can usually be satisfied.

I would like an appetizer.	הָיִיתִי רוֹצֶה מָנָה רִאשׁוֹנָה.		hayiti rotze mana rishona
	אַנְשׁוֹבִי	anshovi	anchovies
	אַסְפָּרָגוּס	asparagus	asparagus tips
	אַרְטִישׁוֹק	artishok	artichokes
	בֵּיצִים	beytzim	eggs
	בֵּיצִים בְּמַיוֹנֶז	beytzim bemayonez	eggs with mayonnaise
	דָג מָלוּחַ	dag maluaḥ	herring
	דָג מָלוּחַ פִילֶה	dag maluaḥ file	salted herring fillets
	זֵיתִים	zeytim	olives
	חֲמוּצִים	hamutzim	pickled vegetables
	כָּבֵד אַוָז	kaved avaz	goose liver
	כָּבֵד עוֹף	kaved of	chicken liver
	מִיץ פֵּרוֹת	mitz peyrot	fruit juice
	מֶלוֹן	melon	melon
	נַקְנִיק	naknik	salami
	נַקְנִיקִיוֹת	naknikiyot	sausages
	סַרְדִינִים	sardinim	sardines
	סַרְטָנִים	sartanim	lobster
	פַּשְׁטִידָה	pashtida	pâté
	צְדָפוֹת	tzedafot	oysters
	קַוְיָר	kavyar	caviar
	קְצִיצַת עֵגֶל	ketzitzat egel	veal loaf
	שַׁבְּלוּלִים	shablulim	snails

EATING OUT

Israeli specialities

חוּמוּס (humus)	A spicy paste made with ground chick peas and sharp spices
טְחִינָה (teḥina)	A sauce made with ground sesame seeds
אֲבוֹקָדוֹ (avokado)	Avocado; prepared in many different ways
פִּלְפֵּל מְמֻלָּא (pilpel memula)	Pepper stuffed with rice or chopped meat

Salads

What salads do you have?	אֵיזֶה סָלָטִים יֵשׁ לָכֶם?	eyze salatim yesh lakhem
Can you recommend a local speciality?	אַתָּה יָכוֹל לְהַמְלִיץ עַל מַשֶּׁהוּ מְיֻחָד?	ata yakhol lehamlitz al mashehu meyuhad
	סָלָט מְלַפְפוֹנִים	salat melafefonim	cucumber salad
	סָלָט יְרָקוֹת	salat yerakot	green salad
	סָלָט חַסָּה	salat ḥasa	lettuce salad
	סָלָט תַּפּוּחֵי אֲדָמָה	salat tapuhey adama	potato salad
	סָלָט עַגְבָנִיּוֹת	salat agvaniyot	tomato salad
	סָלָט מְעֹרָב	salat meorav	mixed salad

Soup

Soup and fish are traditionally first courses in Jewish meals. There are a few well-known specialities such as *borscht* and chicken soup with *kneidlach*. Israeli restaurants provide a wide variety of soups including European and American specialities. During your trip you'll surely find the following soups on your menu:

I'd like some soup.	אֲנִי רוֹצֶה מָרָק.	ani rotze marak
What do you recommend?	מַה אַתָה מַצִּיעַ?	ma ata matzia
מָרַק אוֹרֶז	marak orez	rice soup
מָרַק אַסְפָּרָגוּס	marak asparagus	asparagus soup
מָרַק בָּצָל	marak batzal	onion soup
מָרַק בָּשָׂר	marak basar	meat soup
מָרַק יְרָקוֹת	marak yerakot	vegetable soup
מָרַק עַגְבָנִיּוֹת	marak agvaniyot	tomato soup
מָרַק עוֹף	marak of	chicken soup
מָרַק פִּטְרִיּוֹת	marak pitriyot	mushroom soup
מָרַק שְׁעוּעִית	marak sheuit	bean soup
מָרַק תַּפּוּחֵי אֲדָמָה	marak tapuhey adama	potato soup
חֲמִיצָה	hamitza	borsht

Of course, you'll doubtless find seaweed soup in a Chinese restaurant, *soupe à l'oignon* in a French restaurant and *chorba* in a Hungarian restaurant.

Meat

What kinds of meat do you have?	אֵיזֶה בָּשָׂר יֵשׁ לָכֶם?	eyze basar yesh lakhem
I'd like some . . .	אֲנִי רוֹצֶה בָּשָׂר . . .	ani rotze besar
beef/pork/veal/ mutton	בָּקָר / חֲזִיר / עֵגֶל / כֶּבֶשׂ	bakar/hazir/egel/keves
	כָּבֵד	kaved	liver
	כַּדּוּרֵי בָּשָׂר	kadurey basar	meat balls
	כְּלָיוֹת	kelayot	kidneys
	לֵב	lev	heart
	לָשׁוֹן	lashon	tongue
	נַקְנִיקִיּוֹת	naknikiyot	sausages
	סְטֵייק	steak	steak
	פִילֶה	file	fillet
	קְצִיצוֹת	ketzitzot	minced (chopped) meat
	קֻרְקְבָנִים	kurkevanim	giblets
	רֶגֶל קְרוּשָׁה	regel kerusha	calf's foot jelly
	רֵאוֹת	reyot	lungs
	שְׁנִיצֶל	shnitzel	schnitzel, veal scallop

How do you like your meat?

barbecued	עַל הָאֵשׁ	al haesh
boiled	מְבֻשָּׁל	mevushal
fried	מְטֻגָּן	metugan
grilled	בַּגְרִיל	bigrill
roasted	צָלוּי	tzaluy
stewed	מְאֻדֶּה	meude
stuffed	מְמֻלָּא	memula
underdone (rare)	מְבֻשָּׁל פָּחוֹת מִדַּי	mevushal pahot miday
medium	בֵּינוֹנִי	beynoni
well-done	מְבֻשָּׁל הֵיטֵב	mevushal heytev

EATING OUT

Israeli meat dishes

Israeli people come from 92 different countries and they've conserved the culinary habits of the diaspora. That's the reason why in Israel you'll find cooking from around the world and an international gastronomic vocabulary.

We recommend you to have . . . אֲנַחְנוּ מַמְלִיצִים עַל . . . *anahnu mamlitzim al*

חַמִין
(hamin)
tchoulent: stuffed tripe, beef and beans; a traditional Jewish dish, specially for the sabbath

קְרֶפְלָךְ
(kreplakh)
kreplach: dough envelopes with a savoury filling

מֵעַיִם
(meayim)
kishke: beef tripe with a flour and shortening filling

שַׁוַּארְמָה
(shawarma)
shawarma: a thick chunk of lamb grilled on a vertical spit, very popular in Israel

קַבָּב
(kabab)
kabab: spiced ground meat grilled on wood fire

שַׁשְׁלִיק
(shashlik)
shashlik: pieces of meat (beef or lamb) grilled on a skewer over wood fire

שַׁקְשׁוּקָה
(shakshuka)
shakshuka: a meat and potato casserole

Note: Most dishes are eaten with pickled vegetables (*hamu-tzim*).

EATING OUT

Fish

Fish dishes are very popular in Israel. Gefilte fish is the local favourite.

I would like some fish.   דָּג, בְּבַקָשָׁה.   dag, bevakasha

אַמְנוּן	amnun	"Saint Peter's fish"
בַּקָלָה	bakala	hake
דָּג מָלוּחַ קָצוּץ	dag maluaḥ katzutz	herring, chopped
טוּנָה	tuna	tunny, tuna
סַרְדִּינִים	sardinim	sardines
פִילֶה	file	fillet
קַרְפִּיוֹן	karpion	carp
שְׁפְרוֹטִים	shprotim	sprats

דַּג מְמֻלָּא
(dag memula)
Gefilte fish, made of chopped carp, onion and spices. The stuffing is enveloped in the carp skin.

Shellfish is non-kosher. You can have lobster and crayfish in several non-kosher restaurants in the coastal area.

There are many ways of preparing fish. Here are the Hebrew translations of the ways you may want it served:

baked	אָפוּי	afuy
fried	מְטֻגָּן	metugan
grilled	בְּגְרִיל	bigrill
marinated	כָּבוּש	kavush
poached	מְבֻשָּׁל	mevushal
smoked	מְעֻשָּׁן	meushan
stewed	מְאֻדֶּה	meude

Fowl

Aviculture is a highly developed field in Israel. Many kinds of chicken dishes are offered.

I'd like some fowl.	אֲנִי רוֹצֶה עוֹף.	ani rotze of
What poultry dishes do you serve?	מַה אַתָּה מַצִּיעַ?	ma ata matzia

עוֹף	of	chicken
עוֹף מְמֻלָּא	of memula	stuffed chicken
כָּנָף	kanaf	wing
עוֹף צָלוּי	of tzaluy	grilled chicken
קֻרְקְבָנִים	kurkevanim	chicken giblets
כָּבֵד עוֹף	kaved of	chicken liver
רֶגֶל עוֹף	regel of	chicken leg
חָזֶה עוֹף	haze of	chicken breast
תַּרְנְגוֹל הֹדוּ	tarnegol hodu	turkey
בַּרְוָז	barvaz	duck

Vegetables and seasonings

What vegetables do you recommend?	עַל אֵיזֶה יְרָקוֹת אַתָּה מַמְלִיץ?	al eyze yerakot ata mamlitz
I'd prefer some salad.	אֲנִי מַעֲדִיף סָלָט.	ani maadif salat

אַסְפָּרָגוּס	asparagus	asparagus
אֲפוּנָה	afuna	peas
אֹרֶז	orez	rice
אַרְטִישׁוֹק	artishok	artichokes
בָּצָל	batzal	onions
גֶּזֶר	gezer	carrots
חַסָּה	hasa	lettuce

חֲצִילִים	hatzilim	eggplant (aubergine)
חַרְדָּל	hardal	mustard
כְּרוּב	keruv	cabbage
כְּרוּבִית	keruvit	cauliflower
מְלָפְפוֹן	melafefon	cucumber
מְלָפְפוֹן חָמוּץ	melafefon ḥamutz	gherkins (pickles)
סֶלֶק	selek	beetroot
עַגְבָנִיּוֹת	agvaniyot	tomatoes
עֲדָשִׁים	adashim	lentils
פֶּטְרוֹזִילְיָה	petrozilia	parsley
פִּטְרִיּוֹת	pitriyot	mushrooms
פִּלְפְּלִים	pilpelim	sweet peppers
צְנוֹן	tzenon	radish
קִשּׁוּאִים	kishuim	marrow (zucchini)
שׁוּם	shum	garlic
שְׁעוּעִית	sheuit	kidney beans
תִּירָס	tiras	maize (corn)
תַּפּוּחֵי־אֲדָמָה	tapuḥey adama	potatoes
תֶּרֶד	tered	spinach

Vegetables may be served:

baked	אָפוּי	afuy
boiled	מְבֻשָּׁל	mevushal
chopped	קָצוּץ	katzutz
creamed	בְּשַׁמֶּנֶת	beshamenet
diced	חָתוּךְ	ḥatukh
fried	מְטֻגָּן	metugan
grilled	בַּגְּרִיל	bigrill
roasted	צָלוּי	tzaluy
stewed	מְאֻדֶּה	meude
stuffed	מְמֻלָּא	memula

Dairy products

One of the principal rules laid down in the kosher law is a strict separation of dairy products and meat. They can't be eaten together.

You won't find such a wide variety of cheese in Israel as you may be used to at home. On the other hand, there's a large choice of sour milk and yogurt. And, of course, you will encounter the best known names in cheese such as camembert, roquefort, limburger, etc. There are a few basic expressions you may want to use:

white cheese	גְּבִינָה לְבָנָה	gevina levana
yellow cheese	גְּבִינָה צְהֻבָּה	gevina tzehuba
salt cheese	גְּבִינָה מְלוּחָה	gevina meluḥa

Note: You'll find a wide selection of tasty cheeses made from sheep's milk.

שַׁמֶּנֶת (shamenet)	sour cream
אֶשֶׁל (eshel)	sour milk, very popular in Israel; today it comes in assorted flavours
לֶבֶּן (leben)	a kind of yogurt

Obviously, butter with or after a meat dish is taboo, but you can ask for margarine.

| butter | חֶמְאָה | ḥema |
| margarine | מַרְגָּרִינָה | margarina |

Fruit

Fruit is Israel's most common dessert. Owing to its geographical situation, Israel can provide a very wide selection of fruit, both tropical and European.

Have you got fresh fruit?	יֵשׁ לָכֶם פֵּירוֹת טְרִיִּים?	yesh lakhem peyrot triim
	אֲבַטִּיחַ	avatiaḥ	watermelon
	אֱגוֹזִים	egozim	nuts
	אַגָּס	agas	pear
	אֲנוֹנָה	anona	anona (custard apple)
	אֲנָנָס	ananas	pineapple
	אֲפַרְסֵק	afarsek	peach
	אֶשְׁכּוֹלִית	eshkolit	grapefruit
	בָּנָנָה	banana	banana
	לִימוֹן	limon	lemon
	דֻּבְדְּבָנִים	duvdevanim	cherries
	מֶלוֹן	melon	melon
	מַנְגּוֹ	mango	mango
	מַנְדָּרִינָה / קְלֶמַנְטִינָה	mandarina/klementina	tangerine
	מִשְׁמֵשׁ	mishmesh	apricot
	עֲנָבִים	anavim	grapes
	פֶּטֶל	petel	raspberries
	צִמּוּקִים	tzimukim	raisins
	רִמּוֹנִים	rimonim	pomegranates
	שְׁזִיף	shezif	plum
	שְׁקֵדִים	shekedim	almonds
	תְּאֵנִים	teenim	figs
	תּוּת שָׂדֶה	tut sade	strawberries
	תְּמָרִים	temarim	dates
	תַּפּוּז	tapuz	orange
	תַּפּוּחַ עֵץ	tapuaḥ etz	apple

EATING OUT

Seeds

One of Israel's national "sports" is cracking sunflower seeds.
They're sold everywhere, especially near stadiums, cinemas
and public places. So don't be surprised if you hear strange
sounds while you're watching a movie.

seeds	גַּרְעִינִים	garinim

Dessert

If you have survived all the courses on the menu, you may
want to say:

I'd like a dessert, please.	אֲבַקֵּשׁ מָנָה אַחֲרוֹנָה.	avakesh mana aharona
Something light, please.	מַשֶּׁהוּ קַל, בְּבַקָּשָׁה.	mashehu kal, bevakasha
Just a small portion.	לֹא הַרְבֵּה, בְּבַקָּשָׁה.	lo harbe, bevakasha
Nothing more, thanks.	זֶה הַכֹּל, תּוֹדָה.	ze hakol, toda

If you're not sure what to order, ask the waiter:

What have you for dessert?	מַה יֵשׁ לָכֶם לְמָנָה אַחֲרוֹנָה?	ma yesh lakhem lemana aharona
What do you recommend?	מַה אַתָּה מַצִּיעַ?	ma ata matzia
ice-cream	גְּלִידָה	gelida
cake	עוּגָה	uga
biscuits (cookies)	עוּגִיּוֹת	ugiyot
compote	לִפְתָּן	liftan
fruit	פֵּירוֹת	peyrot

The bill (check)

May I have the bill (check), please?	חֶשְׁבּוֹן, בְּבַקָשָׁה!	heshbon, bevakasha
Haven't you made a mistake?	אֵין טָעוּת?	en taut
Is service included?	זֶה כּוֹלֵל שֵׁרוּת?	ze kolel sherut
Is everything included?	זֶה כּוֹלֵל הַכֹּל?	ze kolel hakol
Do you accept traveller's cheques?	אַתֶם מְקַבְּלִים הַמְחָאוֹת נוֹסְעִים?	atem makablim hamhaot nosim
Thank you, this is for you.	תוֹדָה, זֶה בִּשְׁבִילְךָ.	toda, ze bishvilkha
Keep the change.	הָעוֹדֶף בִּשְׁבִילְךָ.	haodef bishvilkha
That was a very good meal. We enjoyed it, thank you.	הָיְתָה אֲרוּחָה נֶהֱדֶרֶת. נֶהֱנֵינוּ מְאֹד, תוֹדָה רַבָּה.	hayta aruha nehederet. nehneynu meod, toda raba
We'll come again some time.	לְהִתְרָאוֹת.	lehitraot

```
כולל שרות
SERVICE INCLUDED
```

Complaints

But perhaps you'll have something to complain about ...

That's not what I ordered, I asked for ...	זֶה לֹא מַה שֶׁרָצִיתִי, בִּקַשְׁתִי ...	ze lo ma sheratziti, bikashti
I don't like this/I can't eat this.	זֶה לֹא מוֹצֵא חֵן בְּעֵינַי, לֹא אוּכַל לֶאֱכוֹל אֶת זֶה.	ze lo motze hen beeynay lo ukhal leekhol et ze
May I change this?	אֶפְשָׁר לְהַחְלִיף אֶת זֶה?	efshar lehahlif et ze
The meat is ...	הַבָּשָׂר ...	habasar
overdone	יוֹתֵר מִדַי מְבֻשָׁל	yoter miday mevushal
underdone	פָּחוֹת מִדַי מְבוּשָׁל	pahot miday mevushal
too tough	יוֹתֵר מִדַי קָשֶׁה	yoter miday kashe

This is too . . .	יוֹתֵר מִדַּי...	yoter miday
bitter/salty/sweet	מַר / מָלוּחַ / מָתוֹק	mar/maluaḥ/matok
The food is cold.	הָאֹכֶל קַר.	haokhel kar
This isn't fresh.	זֶה לֹא טָרִי.	ze lo tari
Would you ask the head waiter to come over?	קְרָא, בְּבַקָּשָׁה, לַמֶּלְצַר הָרָאשִׁי.	kera, bevakasha, lameltzar harashi

Drinks

Wine

Israel's vineyards produce a large selection of wines, most of them sweet. But you'll find also excellent dry wines. Here are some of the best:

Adom Atic	slightly sweet red
Avdat	dry red
Vin Fou	red
Rose of Carmel	slightly sweet rosé
Château de la Montagne	white
Carmel Hock	slightly sweet white

red	אָדוֹם	adom
white	לָבָן	lavan
dry	יָבֵשׁ	yavesh
sparkling	תּוֹסֵס	toses
sweet	מָתוֹק	matok

I'd like . . . of . . .	אֲבַקֵּשׁ . . .	avakesh
a bottle	בַּקְבּוּק שֶׁל . . .	bakbuk shel
half a bottle	חֲצִי בַּקְבּוּק	hatzi bakbuk
a glass	כּוֹס	kos
I'd like something . . .	הָיִיתִי רוֹצֶה מַשֶּׁהוּ . . .	hayiti rotze mashehu
sweet/sparkling/dry	מָתוֹק / תּוֹסֵס / יָבֵשׁ	matok/toses/yavesh
I want a bottle of white wine.	אֲנִי רוֹצֶה בַּקְבּוּק יַיִן לָבָן.	ani rotze bakbuk yayin lavan
I don't want anything too sweet.	לֹא יוֹתֵר מִדַּי מָתוֹק.	lo yoter miday matok
How much is a bottle of . . . ?	כַּמָּה עוֹלֶה בַּקְבּוּק . . . ?	kama ole bakbuk
Haven't you anything cheaper?	אֵין מַשֶּׁהוּ יוֹתֵר זוֹל?	en mashehu yoter zol
Fine, that will do.	טוֹב מְאֹד, זֶהוּ זֶה.	tov meod; zehu ze

If you enjoyed the wine, you may want to say:

Bring me another . . . please.	תָּבִיא לִי עוֹד . . . , בְּבַקָּשָׁה.	tavi li od . . . bevakasha
glass/bottle	כּוֹס / בַּקְבּוּק	kos/bakbuk
What is the name of this wine?	אֵיךְ קוֹרְאִים לַיַּיִן הַזֶּה?	ekh korim layayin haze
Where does this wine come from?	מֵאֵיפֹה בָּא הַיַּיִן הַזֶּה?	meeyfo ba hayayin haze
How old is this wine?	בֶּן כַּמָּה הַיַּיִן הַזֶּה?	ben kama hayayin haze

glass	כּוֹס	kos
bottle	בַּקְבּוּק	bakbuk

Beer and liquor

Bartending has retained its international vocabulary in Israel. Perhaps you wish to order one of the following on some occasion or another, although you mustn't expect to find such a wide choice everywhere.

beer	בִּירָה	bira
malt beer	בִּירָה שְׁחוֹרָה (מאלְץ)	bira sheḥora (maltz)
brandy, cognac	קוֹנְיַאק	konyak
gin	ג׳ִין	gin
gin and tonic	ג׳ִין וְטוֹנִיק	gin vetonik
vodka	וֹדְקָה	vodka
whisky	וִיסְקִי	whisky
whisky and soda	וִיסְקִי עִם סוֹדָה	whisky im soda
neat (straight)	נָקִי	naki
on the rocks	עִם קֶרַח	im keraḥ
double	כָּפוּל	kaful

But you should take this opportunity to taste *arak*, rice liquor available in 80 and 100 percent proof. A wide variety of fruit-flavoured liquors exist. Try:

Carmel Mizraḥi 777	שֶׁבַע־שֶׁבַע־שֶׁבַע	sheva-sheva-sheva
I'd like to taste arak, please.	הָיִיתִי רוֹצֶה לִטְעֹם קְצָת אָרָק, בְּבַקָשָׁה.	hayiti rotze litom ketzat arak, bevakasha
Bring me a glass of brandy, please.	תָבִיא לִי כּוֹסִית קוֹנְיַק, בְּבַקָשָׁה.	tavi li kosit konyak, bevakasha

לְחַיִים!
(leḥayim)
CHEERS!

Other beverages

Gazoz (soft drink) is the most popular soft drink. It's sold at every refreshment stand.

gazoz	גָזוֹז	gazoz
sweet	מָתוֹק	matok
sour	חָמוּץ	hamutz
I'd like a . . .	אֲבַקֵּשׁ...	avakesh
Have you any . . . ?	יֵשׁ לָכֶם...?	yesh lakhem
chocolate	קָקָאוֹ	kakao
coffee	קָפֶה	kafe
cup of coffee	סֵפֶל קָפֶה	sefel kafe
coffee with cream	קָפֶה הָפוּךְ	kafe hafukh
expresso coffee	אֶסְפְּרֶסוֹ	espresso
iced coffee	קָפֶה קַר	kafe kar
black coffee	קָפֶה שָׁחוֹר	kafe shahor
Turkish coffee	קָפֶה טוּרְקִי	kafe turki
fruit juice	מִיץ פֵּרוֹת	mitz peyrot
grapefruit	אֶשְׁכּוֹלִיוֹת	eshkoliyot
lemon/orange	לִימוֹן / תַפּוּזִים	limon/tapuzim
pineapple/tomato/	אַנָס / עַגְבָנִיוֹת /	ananas/agvaniyot/
carrot	גֶזֶר	gezer
lemonade	לִימוֹנָדָה	limonada
milk	חָלָב	halav
milk shake	מִילק שֵׁייק	milk shake
mineral water	מַיִם מִינֶרָלִיים	mayim mineraliim
orangeade	אוֹרַנְג׳דָה	orangeada
soda water	כּוֹס סוֹדָה	kos soda
sugar	סוּכָּר	sukar
tea with milk/lemon	תֵה עִם חָלָב / לִימוֹן	te im halav/limon

Eating light—Snacks

Israel's most popular snack is *falafel*. Its basic ingredients are small balls of ground chick peas, fried and served in *pita*. This is an oriental kind of bread: round, flat, and hollow.

I'll have one of those, please.	תֵּן לִי אֶחָד כָּזֶה, בְּבַקָּשָׁה.	ten li eḥad kaze, bevakasha
To the left/to the right/above/below.	מִשְּׂמֹאל / מִיָּמִין / לְמַעְלָה / לְמַטָּה.	mismol/miyamin/ lemaala/lemata
Give me a/an/ some . . ., please.	תֵּן לִי . . ., בְּבַקָּשָׁה.	ten li . . ., bevakasha
biscuits (cookies)	עוּגִיּוֹת	ugiyot
bread	לֶחֶם	leḥem
butter	חֶמְאָה	ḥema
cake	עוּגָה	uga
chocolate	שׁוֹקוֹלָד	shokolad
chewing gum	מַסְטִיק	mastik
falafel	פָלָפֶל	falafel
hamburger	הַמְבּוּרְגֶר	hamburger
hot-dog	נַקְנִיקִיָּה חַמָּה	naknikiya ḥama
ice-cream	גְּלִידָה	gelida
roll	לַחְמָנִיָּה	laḥmaniya
salad	סָלָט	salat
sandwich	סֶנְדְּבִיץ'	sandwich
sweets	סוּכָּרִיּוֹת	sukariyot
toast	טוֹסְט	tost
waffles	וַפְלִים	vaflim
How much is that?	כַּמָּה זֶה עוֹלֶה?	kama ze ole

בְּתֵאָבוֹן
(beteavon)
BON APPETIT!

Arab cooking

Food is prepared pretty much alike throughout the Middle East. Arab cooking in Israel, however, is particularly influenced by the Circassians, a Moslem people who migrated in the last century from Russia. Doubtless, the best known of their dishes is chicken Circassian (*cherkess taug* شركس طوج) which is minced chicken baked with rice and seasoned vegetables.

Appetizers, salads, soup

You'll find *falafel*, *hommos* and *tahina* (explained earlier in this section) in Arab restaurants but other appetizers as well that are nearly always served with Arab bread (*khubez arabi*). Made of wheat and cornflour, this tasty, flat, round bread replaces eating utensils as it's used to scoop up food right from the bowl or plate. Try these preparations, too, with *khubez*:

تبوله (tabuleh)	A Lebanese salad of chopped tomatoes, lettuce, onions, mint leaves, cracked wheat and bread crumbs all marinated in salad dressing. This may be scooped up either with *khubez* or lettuce leaves.
فول مدمس (ful medames)	An Egyptian dish of baked black beans seasoned with oil, lemon juice, caraway seeds
خيار باللبن (khiar bilaban)	Minced cucumbers in yoghurt, flavoured with garlic and ground mint leaves; served cold, it's a most refreshing salad on a hot summer day.

Or these dishes:

صلاطة ملفوف (salatet malfuf)	coleslaw
قرنبيط مقلي (karnabit makli)	fried cauliflower
فته (fata)	mutton and vegetable soup served with bread crumbs

Main dishes

Chicken, lamb and mutton are most commonly used in countless preparations which are virtually always accompanied by a dish of well-prepared rice. Fish may be ordered in coastal areas but other seafood is rarely found in restaurants.

Like kosher law, that of the Moslem faith also forbids eating pork. A favourite vegetable dish combines vegetable marrow (zucchini), eggplant and cauliflower braised with tomatoes, onions and garlic in melted butter or fried in oil.

منسف (mansaf)	Seasoned, boiled rice garnished with boiled chunks of mutton, topped with a butter sauce; this bedouin dish is served on Arab bread.	
سفيحا (sfiḥa)	A pastry crust garnished with seasoned minced mutton	
مدفون (madfun)	Layers of eggplant, minced meat or chicken, onion, rice; baked with tomato-sauce and grated cheese, flavoured with spices	
سمكه حاره (samake hara)	Marinated sea bass stuffed with fresh chili peppers, finely-minced onion, parsley, pomegranates, minced nuts; grilled	
كباب (kabab)	This well-known style of cooking nearly always consists of chunks of lamb and/or mutton seasoned with parsley and ground pepper; charcoal grilled.	
مسخن (musakhan)	Grilled chicken, served on bread with oil, chili peppers onions	
كدره (kidreh)	Lamb chops baked with rice and butter	
مقلوبه (maklubeh)	Rice with meat and cauliflower or eggplant	

كبّة	This dish from Syria and Lebanon consists of minced
(kibeh)	mutton, cracked wheat, onion, nutmeg; formed into a patty and served either:

كبّة نايه	raw (like beef tartare)
(kibeh nayeh)	

كبّة بالصنيه	baked
(kibeh bisenieh)	

كبّة لبنيه	or rolled into balls, served with goat milk soup
(kibeh labnieh)	

You can order many types of vegetable, poultry or meat dishes stuffed with seasoned mutton or other minced meat, rice and a tomato or lemon sauce. Try some of these preparations which also reflect Lebanese, Syrian or Turkish cooking:

كوسا محشي	kusa mahshi	stuffed vegetable marrow (zucchini)
باذنجان محشي	batinjan mahshi	stuffed eggplant
بندوره محشي	bandora mahshi	stuffed tomatoes
ورق عنب محشي	warak inab mahshi	stuffed vine leaves
حمام محشي	haman mahshi	stuffed pigeons
دجاج محشي	djaj mahshi	stuffed chicken
خاروف محشي	kharuf mahshi	stuffed lamb

Desserts

Desserts are generally taken with a cup of coffee between meals and not so much as a last course like in America or Britain. Arab desserts are usually very sweet, baked in melted butter and topped with a honey syrup. Among some of the popular sweet dishes are:

كنافه	crushed almonds, pistachio or other nuts enclosed in a
(kunafa)	mesh of pastry fibres; fried in melted butter and topped with honey syrup (Syria)

بقــلاوة (baklava)	crushed almonds, pistachios or other nuts wrapped in paper-thin layers of dough, baked in melted butter and topped with honey syrup (Turkey and Lebanon)
بـبـوسه basbuse	semolina cake containing melted butter, crushed almonds, served in syrup (Egypt)
مهلبيــه (muhalabieh)	rice pudding (Turkey)
كازان ديبي (kazan dibi)	pudding with caramelized bottom, served with syrup (Turkey)

EATING OUT

Beverages

While aperitifs and cocktails are largely unknown and wine is scarcely served in Arab restaurants, *bira* (beer) or *arak* (aniseed liqueur) may be ordered with a meal.

Only Arabic or Turkish coffee (*kahve*) will be offered in Arabic restaurants. You may order it *mazbut* (medium sweet) or *sukar ziadah* (sweet). Don't forget that Arab coffee is quite strong but generally well brewed. When the coffee is served—grounds and all—let it sit a minute so that the grounds can settle to the bottom of the cup, and then sip only half the cup.

شاي	chay	tea
ختميه	khitmieh	bedouin tea (with herbs)
شراب	sharab	syrup
جزوز	gazoz	carbonated water
جزوز لمون	gazoz lamun	lemon drink
جزوز برتقال	gazoz bortokal	orangeade, orange squash
حليب	halib	milk

Travelling around

Plane

Most principal cities in Israel as well as many vacation resorts are served by domestic airlines. At any airport you're sure to find someone who speaks English. But here are a few airborne expressions you may want to know . . .

Do you speak English?	אַתָּה מְדַבֵּר אַנְגְלִית?	ata medaber anglit
Is there a flight to Haifa?	יֵשׁ טִיסָה לְחֵיפָה?	yesh tisa leHaifa
When's the next plane to Eilat?	מָתַי הַטִּיסָה הַבָּאָה לְאֵילַת?	matay hatisa habaa leEilat
Can I make a connection to Jerusalem?	הַאִם יִהְיֶה לִי קֶשֶׁר לִירוּשָׁלַיִם?	haim ihye li kesher liYerushalaim
I'd like a ticket to Haifa.	אֲבַקֵּשׁ כַּרְטִיס לְחֵיפָה.	avakesh kartis leHaifa
What's the fare to Tel Aviv?	כַּמָּה עוֹלָה הַטִּיסָה לְתֵל־אָבִיב?	kama ola hatisa leTel-Aviv
single (one-way)	בְּכִוּוּן אֶחָד	bekhivun ehad
return (roundtrip)	הָלוֹךְ וָחֲזוֹר	halokh vehazor
What time does the plane take off?	מָתַי מַמְרִיא הַמָּטוֹס?	matay mamri hamatos
What time do I have to check in?	מָתַי עָלַי לִהְיוֹת בְּמָקוֹם?	matay alay lihyot bamakom
What's the flight number?	מָה מִסְפַּר הַטִּיסָה?	ma mispar hatisa
What time do we arrive?	מָתַי נַגִּיעַ?	matay nagia

Bus—Coach

Buses are the most important means of transport in Israel. In all buses you pay as you enter. There are two sorts of bus lines: city buses and inter-urban buses. Inter-urban buses run two kinds of services: fast and slow.

It's not recommendable to travel by bus in the cities during rush hours. In Tel Aviv especially, buses can be very crowded. It might be better (though more expensive) to try *sherut* or taxi services. However, in order to make transportation easier, a few companies have decided to run small mini-buses on the same lines as those run by the public cooperative lines. Again, don't forget: there's complete non-activity on Saturdays (except in Haifa and its suburban area).

Enquiries

I'd like a bus pass.	אֲבַקֵשׁ כַּרְטִיס.	avakesh kartis.
Where can I get a bus to Tel Aviv?	אֵיפֹה יֵשׁ אוֹטוֹבּוּס לְתֵל־אָבִיב?	eyfo yesh otobus leTel-Aviv
What bus do I take to Haifa?	אֵיזֶה אוֹטוֹבּוּס אֲנִי צָרִיךְ לְחֵיפָה?	eyze otobus ani tzarikh leHaifa
Where's the . . . ?	אֵיפֹה . . . ?	eyfo
bus station	הַתַּחֲנָה הַמֶּרְכָּזִית	hataḥana hamerkazit
bus stop	תַּחֲנַת הָאוֹטוֹבּוּס	taḥanat haotobus
terminal	הַתַּחֲנָה הָאַחֲרוֹנָה	hataḥana haaḥarona
When's the . . . bus to Beer Sheba?	מָתַי יוֹצֵא הָאוֹטוֹבּוּס הַ . . . לִבְאֵר שֶׁבַע?	matay yotze haotobus ha . . . liBeer Sheva
first/last/next	רִאשׁוֹן / אַחֲרוֹן / בָּא	rishon/aḥaron/ba
How often do the buses to Haifa run?	כָּל כַּמָּה זְמַן יֵשׁ אוֹטוֹבּוּס לְחֵיפָה?	kol kama zeman yesh otobus leHaifa

FOR TAXI, see page 27

| Do I have to change buses? | צָרִיךְ לְהַחֲלִיף אוֹטוֹבּוּס? | tzarikh lehaḥlif otobus |
| How long does the journey take? | כַּמָה זְמַן נִמְשֶׁכֶת הַנְסִיעָה? | kama zeman nimshekhet hanesia |

Timetables

If you intend to do a lot of bus travel, it might be a good idea to buy a timetable. These are based on the 24-hour clock and are for sale at ticket offices, information desks and in some bookshops.

| I'd like to buy a timetable. | אֲנִי רוֹצֶה לִקְנוֹת לוּחַ זְמַנִים. | ani rotze liknot luaḥ zemanim |

Tickets

Where's the . . . ?	אֵיפֹה . . . ?	eyfo
information office	הַמוֹדִיעִין	hamodiin
ticket office	הַקוּפָּה	hakupa
I want a ticket to Haifa, single (one-way)/ return (roundtrip).	אֲנִי רוֹצֶה כַּרְטִיס לְחֵיפָה, כִּיוּן אֶחָד / הָלוֹךְ וְחָזוֹר.	ani rotze kartis leḤaifa, kivun eḥad/halokh vehazor
I'd like two singles to Jerusalem.	אֲנִי רוֹצֶה שְׁנֵי כַּרְטִיסִים לִירוּשָׁלַיִם.	ani rotze sheney kartisim liYerushalaim
How much is the fare to Beer Sheba?	כַּמָה עוֹלָה הַנְסִיעָה לִבְאֵר-שֶׁבַע?	kama ola hanesia liBeer-Sheva
Is it half price for a child? He's 13.	יְלָדִים מְשַׁלְמִים חֲצִי מְחִיר? הוּא בֶּן 13.	yeladim meshalmim ḥatzi meḥir? hu ben 13

Note: Children up to the age of 5 travel free.

Possible answers

כִּוּוּן אֶחָד אוֹ הָלוֹךְ וְחָזוֹר?	Single or return (one-way or roundtrip)?
עַד גִּיל . . . חֲצִי מְחִיר.	It's half price up to the age of . . .
צָרִיךְ לְשַׁלֵּם מְחִיר מָלֵא.	You'll have to pay full fare.

All aboard

Excuse me. May I get by?	סְלִיחָה, אֶפְשָׁר לַעֲבוֹר?	seliḥa, efshar laavor
Is this seat taken?	הַמָּקוֹם הַזֶּה תָּפוּס?	hamakom haze tafus
Is this seat free?	הַמָּקוֹם הַזֶּה פָּנוּי?	hamakom haze panuy

> אסור לעשן
> NO SMOKING

I think that's my seat.	סְלִיחָה, זֶה הַמָּקוֹם שֶׁלִּי.	seliḥa, ze hamakom sheli
Can you tell me when we get to Jerusalem?	מָתַי נַגִּיעַ לִירוּשָׁלַיִם?	matay nagia liYerushalaim
What station is this?	אֵיךְ נִקְרָא הַמָּקוֹם הַזֶּה?	ekh nikra hamakom haze
Will you tell me when to get off?	תּוּכַל לְהַגִּיד לִי מָתַי לָרֶדֶת?	tukhal lehagid li matay laredet
I want to get off at Herzlyah.	אֲנִי רוֹצֶה לָרֶדֶת בְּהֶרְצְלִיָּה.	ani rotze laredet beHerzlia
Please let me off at the next stop.	עֲצוֹר, בְּבַקָשָׁה, בַּתַחֲנָה הַבָּאָה.	atzor, bevakasha, betaḥana habaa
May I have my luggage, please?	אֶפְשָׁר לְקַבֵּל אֶת הַמִּזְוָדָה שֶׁלִּי?	efshar lekabel et hamizvada sheli

Train

After buses and taxis, trains are the most common means of transport in the country. They operate only between the main cities: Haifa-Tel Aviv, Haifa-Jerusalem, Tel Aviv-Jerusalem and Tel Aviv-Beer Sheba. Sometimes small trains run from Haifa to Naharyah to the north and from Beer Sheba to Dimona to the south. Israeli trains are modern, clean, and comfortable; the longest trip you can make would last about 3 hours (Haifa-Jerusalem), and the most panoramic journey is Tel Aviv-Jerusalem. Israel's railways have a total mileage of 340 miles.

The winter in Israel is so mild that the trains don't need to be heated. The train is also the cheapest means of transportation. Children and groups are entitled to reductions. There are usually enough seats for everyone, except on holiday eves and during rush hours (early in the morning and in the evening). However, seat reservation isn't common. If you don't want to risk a tiring journey, numbered seats are available for reservation.

All passenger services are provided with a buffet car or a buffet service. Yet distances are so short that usually only drinks, snacks, and light meals are served. On Jewish high holy days and from sundown Friday to sundown Saturday trains—like all other public transport—don't move an inch.

To the station

Where's the railway station?	אֵיפֹה תַחֲנַת הָרַכֶּבֶת?	eyfo tahanat harakevet
Taxi, please!	טַקְסִי! מוֹנִית!	taxi! monit
Take me to the railway station.	לְתַחֲנַת הָרַכֶּבֶת, בְּבַקָּשָׁה.	letahanat harakevet, bevakasha
What's the fare?	כַּמָּה זֶה עוֹלֶה?	kama ze ole

Enquiries

How much is the fare to . . . ?	כַּמָּה עוֹלֶה כַּרְטִיס לְ...?	kama ole kartis le
Is it a through train?	זֹאת רַכֶּבֶת יְשִׁירָה?	zot rakevet yeshira
Does the train stop at Herzlyah?	הַאִם הָרַכֶּבֶת עוֹצֶרֶת בְּהֶרְצְלִיָה?	haim harakevet otzeret beHerzlia
When is the . . . train to Haifa?	מָתַי יוֹצֵאת הָרַכֶּבֶת... לְחֵיפָה?	matay yotzet harakevet leHaifa
first/last/next	הָרִאשׁוֹנָה / הָאַחֲרוֹנָה / הַבָּאָה	harishona/haaharona/habaa
What time does the train from Jerusalem arrive?	מָתַי מַגִּיעָה הָרַכֶּבֶת מִירוּשָׁלַיִם?	matay magia harakevet miYerushalaim
What time does the train for Haifa leave?	מָתַי בְּדִיּוּק יוֹצֵאת הָרַכֶּבֶת לְחֵיפָה?	matay bediyuk yotzet harakevet leHaifa
Is the train late?	הָרַכֶּבֶת מִתְאַחֶרֶת?	harakevet mitaheret
Is there a dining-car on the train?	יֵשׁ קְרוֹן־מִסְעָדָה בָּרַכֶּבֶת?	yesh kron-misada barakevet

כניסה	ENTRANCE
יציאה	EXIT
לרציפים	TO THE PLATFORMS

FOR TAXI, see page 27

TRAVELLING AROUND

Platform (track)

What platform does the train for Haifa leave from?	מֵאֵיזֶה רָצִיף יוֹצֵאת הָרַכֶּבֶת לְחֵיפָה?	meeyze ratzif yotzet harakevet leHaifa
What platform does the train from Jerusalem arrive at?	לְאֵיזֶה רָצִיף מַגִּיעָה הָרַכֶּבֶת מִירוּשָׁלַיִם?	leeyze ratzif magia harakevet miYerushalaim
Where is platform 4?	אֵיפֹה רָצִיף מִסְפָּר 4?	eyfo ratzif mispar 4
Is this the right platform for the train to Tel Aviv?	זֶה הָרָצִיף לָרַכֶּבֶת הַיּוֹצֵאת לְתֵל־אָבִיב?	ze haratzif larakevet hayotzet leTel-Aviv

Possible answers

רַכֶּבֶת יְשִׁירָה.	It's a direct train.
צָרִיךְ לְהַחְלִיף רַכֶּבֶת בְּ...	You have to change at ...
מַחְלָקָה רִאשׁוֹנָה אוֹ שְׁנִיָּה?	First or second class?
הָרָצִיף ... נִמְצָא...	Platform ... is ...
שָׁם / לְמַטָּה	over there/downstairs
מִשְׂמֹאל / מִיָּמִין	on the left/on the right
הָרַכֶּבֶת לְ... תֵּצֵא בְּ...	The train to ... will leave at ...
מֵרָצִיף...	... from platform ...

Where's the . . . ?

Where's the . . . ?	אֵיפֹה...?	eyfo
buffet	הַמִּזְנוֹן	hamiznon
restaurant	הַמִּסְעָדָה	hamisada
left luggage office	שְׁמִירַת חֲפָצִים	shemirat ḥafatzim
lost and found office	חֲפָצִים אֲבוּדִים	hafatzim avudim
newsstand	דּוּכַן עִתּוֹנִים	dukhan itonim
waiting room	חֲדַר הַמְתָּנָה	ḥadar hamtana
Where are the toilets?	אֵיפֹה הַנּוֹחִיּוּת?	eyfo hanoḥiyut

FOR TICKETS, see page 67

Eating

Restaurant cars serve only light meals; distances are too short for the passenger to dine en route.

Some time on your train journey the ticket collector (*mevaker kartisim*) will come around and say:

Tickets, please!	כַּרְטִיסִים, בְּבַקָּשָׁה!	kartisim, bevaka**sha**

You may want to ask him:

How long does the train stop here?	כַּמָּה זְמַן נִשְׁאֶרֶת הָרַכֶּבֶת בְּתַחֲנָה זֹאת?	kama zeman nisheret harakevet betahana zot

Lost!

We hope you'll have no need for the following phrases on your trip . . . but just in case:

Where's the lost property office?	אֵיפֹה מִשְׂרַד הַחֲפָצִים הָאֲבוּדִים?	eyfo misrad hahafatzim haavudim
I've lost my . . .	אָבַד לִי . . .	avad li
this morning	הַבֹּקֶר	haboker
yesterday	אֶתְמוֹל	etmol
I lost it on my trip to . . .	זֶה קָרָה בַּנְּסִיעָה לְ . . .	ze kara bansia le
It's very valuable.	זֶה מְאֹד יָקָר.	ze meod yakar

Around and about—Sightseeing

Numerous civilizations have risen and collapsed on the territory that's now the state of Israel. Jerusalem has always been a cradle of spiritual life. The biblical past is present in every inch of its soil.

Israel is what we may call a country of past and future. The (revived) Hebrew language forms the only link between the ancient Bible and the present. It's an implement for maintaining tradition; the Bible becomes not only a prayer book but also a tourist guide and an archeological indicator. Thanks to the Bible, sites have been and are being discovered everywhere in the country. Israel thus offers an extensive scope of the entire history of mankind, starting with human relics over a million years old. This is the most ancient archeological discovery in the Middle East, uncovered in the Jordan Valley.

General

Here we're more concerned with the cultural aspect of life than with entertainment; and, for the moment, with towns, rather than the countryside. If you want a guidebook, ask . . .

Can you recommend a good and handy guide book?	אֶפְשָׁר לְקַבֵּל מַדְרִיךְ טוֹב וְשִׁמּוּשִׁי לְטִיּוּלִים בָּאָרֶץ?	efshar lekabel madrikh tov veshimushi letiyulim baaretz
Is there a tourist office?	יֵשׁ כָּאן לִשְׁכַּת תַּיָרוּת?	yesh kan lishkat tayarut
Where is the tourist information centre?	אֵיפֹה לִשְׁכַּת הַמּוֹדִיעִין לְתַיָרִים?	eyfo lishkat hamodiin letayarim
What are the main points of interest?	מַה כְּדַאי כָּאן לִרְאוֹת?	ma keday kan lirot
Is there an English-speaking guide?	יֵשׁ כָּאן מַדְרִיךְ דוֹבֵר אַנְגְּלִית?	yesh kan madrikh dover anglit

We're only here for . . .	נִשְׁאֵר כָּאן רַק . . .	nishaer kan rak
a few hours	שָׁעוֹת אֲחָדוֹת	shaot aḥadot
a day	יוֹם אֶחָד	yom eḥad
three days	שְׁלוֹשָׁה יָמִים	shelosha yamim
a week	שָׁבוּעַ	shavua
Can you recommend a sightseeing tour?	תּוּכַל לְהַמְלִיץ עַל טִיוּל מְעַנְיֵן?	tukhal lehamlitz al tiyul meanyen
Where does the bus start from?	אֵיפֹה יוֹצֵא הָאוֹטוֹבּוּס?	eyfo yotze haotobus
What bus/tram do we want?	בְּאֵיזֶה אוֹטוֹבּוּס מַגִּיעִים לִנְקֻדַּת הַיְצִיאָה?	beeyze otobus magiim linkudat hayetzia
How much does the tour cost?	כַּמָּה עוֹלֶה הַטִּיוּל?	kama ole hatiyul
What time does the tour start?	בְּאֵיזֶה שָׁעָה יוֹצְאִים?	beeyze shaa yotzim
Where's/Where are the . . . ?	אֵיפֹה כָּאן . . . ?	eyfo kan
antiquities	עַתִּיקוֹת	atikot
art gallery	גָּלֶרְיָה לְאָמָּנוּת	galeria leomanut
artists' quarter	שְׁכוּנַת הָאָמָּנִים	shekhunat haomanim
botanical gardens	גַּן בּוֹטָנִי	gan botani
castle	מְצוּדָה	metzuda
cathedral	קָתֶדְרָלָה	katedrala
cave	מְעָרָה	meara
cemetery	בֵּית קְבָרוֹת	bet kevarot
church	כְּנֵסִיָּה	kenesiya
concert hall	אוּלַם קוֹנְצֶרְטִים	ulam kontzertim
convent	מִנְזָר	minzar
docks	נָמֵל	namal
downtown area	מֶרְכַּז הָעִיר	merkaz hair
exhibition	תַּעֲרוּכָה	taarukha
factory	בֵּית חֲרֹשֶׁת	bet ḥaroshet
fortress	מִבְצָר	mivtzar

fountain	מִזְרָקָה	mizraka
gardens	גַּנִּים	ganim
government offices	מִשְׂרְדֵי מֶמְשָׁלָה	misredey memshala
hospital	בֵּית חוֹלִים	bet holim
Knesset	הַכְּנֶסֶת	hakeneset
lake	אֲגַם	agam
law courts	בֵּית מִשְׁפָּט	bet mishpat
library	סִפְרִיָּה	sifriya
market	שׁוּק	shuk
memorial	מַצֶּבֶת זִכָּרוֹן	matzevet zikaron
mosque	מִסְגָּד	misgad
museum	מוּזֵיאוֹן	muzeon
old city	עִיר עַתִּיקָה	ir atika
opera house	הָאוֹפֵּרָה	haopera
palace	אַרְמוֹן	armon
park	גַּן צִבּוּרִי	gan tziburi
planetarium	מִצְפֵּה כּוֹכָבִים	mitzpe kokhavim
post office	מִשְׂרַד דֹּאַר	misrad doar
shopping centre	מֶרְכָּז קְנִיּוֹת	merkaz keniyot
stadium	אִצְטַדְיוֹן	itztadion
statue	פֶּסֶל	pesel
stock exchange	בּוּרְסָה	bursa
synagogue	בֵּית כְּנֶסֶת	bet keneset
television studios	אוּלְפְּנֵי טֶלֶוִיזְיָה	ulpaney televizia
temple	הֵיכָל	heykhal
tomb	קֶבֶר	kever
tower	מִגְדָּל	migdal
town hall	הָעִירִיָּה	hairiya
university	אוּנִיבֶּרְסִיטָה	universita
walls	חוֹמוֹת הָעִיר הָעַתִּיקָה	homot hair haatika
western wall	כֹּתֶל מַעֲרָבִי	kotel maaravi
zoo	גַּן חַיּוֹת	gan hayot

SIGHTSEEING

FOR CAR RENTAL, see page 26

Admission

Is the . . . open on Saturdays?	הַאִם הַ...פָּתוּחַ בְּשַׁבָּת?	haim ha . . . patuaḥ beshabat
When does it open?	מֵאֵיזֶה שָׁעָה פָּתוּחַ?	meeyze shaa patuaḥ
When does it close?	מָתַי סוֹגְרִים?	matay sogrim
How much is the admission charge?	כַּמָה עוֹלָה הַכְּנִיסָה?	kama ola hakenisa
Is there any reduction for . . . ?	יֵשׁ הֲנָחָה...?	yesh hanaḥa
students/children	לִסְטוּדֶנְטִים / לִילָדִים	listudentim/liyeladim
Here's my ticket.	הִנֵה הַכַּרְטִיס שֶׁלִי.	hine hakartis sheli
Here are our tickets.	הִנֵה הַכַּרְטִיסִים שֶׁלָנוּ.	hine hakartisim shelanu
Have you a guide book in English?	יֵשׁ מַדְרִיךְ כָּתוּב אַנְגְלִית.	yesh madrikh katuv anglit
Can I buy a catalogue?	אֶפְשָׁר לִקְנוֹת קָטָלוֹג?	efshar liknot katalog
Is it all right to take pictures?	מוּתָר לְצַלֵם?	mutar letzalem

כניסה חופשית	ADMISSION FREE
אסור לצלם	NO CAMERAS ALLOWED

Who—What—When?

What's that building?	מַה הַבִּנְיָן הַזֶה?	ma habinyan haze
Who was the . . . ?	מִי הָיָה...?	mi haya
architect	הָאַדְרִיכַל	haadrikhal
painter	הַצַיָר	hatzayar
sculptor	הַפַּסָל	hapasal
Who built it?	מִי בָּנָה אֶת זֶה?	mi bana et ze
Who painted that picture?	מִי צִיֵר אֶת הַתְמוּנָה הַזֹאת?	mi tziyer et hatemuna hazot

When did he live?	מָתַי הוּא חַי?	matay hu ḥay
When was it built?	מָתַי זֶה נִבְנָה?	matay ze nivna
Where's the house where . . . ?	אֵיפֹה הַבַּיִת שֶׁבּוֹ...?	eyfo habait shebo
We're interested in . . .	אֲנַחְנוּ מִתְעַנְיְנִים בְּ...	anaḥnu mitanyenim be
antiques	עַתִּיקוֹת	atikot
archaeology	אַרְכֵיאוֹלוֹגְיָה	archaeologia
art	אָמָנוּת	omanut
botany	בּוֹטָנִיקָה	botanika
ceramics	קֶרָמִיקָה	keramika
coins	מַטְבְּעוֹת	matbeot
furniture	רְהִיטִים	rehitim
geology	גֵּאוֹלוֹגְיָה	geologia
history	הִסְטוֹרְיָה	historia
local crafts	מְלֶאכֶת מַחְשֶׁבֶת מְקוֹמִית	melekhet maḥshevet mekomit
medicine	רְפוּאָה	refua
music	מוּסִיקָה	musika
natural history	מַדָּע	mada
painting	צִיּוּר	tziyur
pottery	קַדָּרוּת	kadarut
sculpture	פִּסּוּל	pisul
zoology	זוֹאוֹלוֹגְיָה	zoologia
Where's the . . . department?	אֵיפֹה הַמַּחְלָקָה לְ...?	eyfo hamaḥlaka le

SIGHTSEEING

Just the adjective you've been looking for . . .

It's . . .	זֶה . . .	ze
amazing	מַפְלִיא	mafli
awful	נוֹרָא	nora
beautiful	יָפֶה	yafe
gloomy	עָצוּב	atzuv
interesting	מְעַנְיֵן	meanyen
magnificent	נִפְלָא	nifla
monumental	כַּבִּיר	kabir
sinister	קוֹדֵר	koder
strange	מוּזָר	muzar
stupendous	נֶהְדָּר	nehedar
superb	יוֹצֵא מִן הַכְּלָל	yotze min haklal
terrible	אָיֹם	ayom
terrifying	מַפְחִיד	mafḥid
tremendous	עָצוּם	atzum
ugly	מְכֹעָר	mekhoar

Church services

In Israel there are many places of worship which you can visit at any time. In a church men are supposed to uncover their heads. When entering a mosque you're supposed to take off your shoes, and in a synagogue you should cover your head.

Is there a/an . . . near here?	?... יֵשׁ בְּקִרְבַת מָקוֹם	yesh bekirvat makom
synagogue	בֵּית כְּנֶסֶת	bet keneset
mosque	מִסְגָּד	misgad
Orthodox church	כְּנֵסִיָּה אוֹרְתוֹדוֹכְסִית	kenesiya ortodoksit
Protestant church	כְּנֵסִיָּה פְּרוֹטֶסְטַנְטִית	knesiya protestantit
Catholic church	כְּנֵסִיָּה קָתוֹלִית	knesiya katolit
At what time are services?	?מָתַי שְׁעַת הַתְּפִילָה	matay sheat hatefila

Shabbat

The Hebrew word *shabbat* means rest. It starts at sundown on Friday and ends on Saturday evening. However, this rest day has a significance which differs widely from our usual Sunday rest.

The Jewish *shabbat* is a purely biblical institution. Not all Jews observe it in the same strict manner. Orthodox Jews, reformists and moderates all display various degrees of religious zeal.

The result, in practice, is a partial cessation of all activity, public as well as private. One may even see orthodox Jews go so far as to stop lighting cigarettes, tuning the TV, driving a car and, of course, suspend all remunerated work. But this is an extremist behaviour which does not affect Israel's general way of life.

Apart from the *shabbat*, Israel recognizes many other religious holy days. Passover commemorates the exodus of the Jews from Egypt. Its observance is ruled by a milleniums-old tradition. Pentecost, according to Jewish law, commemorates the handing down of the Ten Commandments to Moses. The Jewish feast of the Tabernacles represents the harvest holiday. Jewish New Year comes in September or October and, ten days after, a Day of Atonement. On these holidays all public activities come to a total stop. For a complete calendar, see page 181.

see page 181.

Relaxing

Cinema (movies)—Theatre

Cinemas usually give two showings per day. A few have a continuous programme starting at 10 or 11 a.m., mostly showing action movies.

All films are shown in their original version with Hebrew subtitles. Films which aren't in English also carry English subtitles, so you'll have no linguistic problems to solve on that account. For evening showings seats are numbered and it's advisable to make advance reservations.

The Israeli theatre has a good reputation. Performances generally start at 8.30 p.m. However, check curtain time in a newspaper or on a billboard. There's also a weekly guide called "This Week in Israel", where you'll find all information you may need. In the larger cities there are ticket reservation offices selling tickets for all kinds of shows, theatres as well as cinemas. Depending on whether it's the winter or summer season, curtain time may vary from 7 to 9 p.m.

Have you the most recent "This Week in Israel"?	יֵשׁ לְךָ גִּלָּיוֹן אַחֲרוֹן שֶׁל "This Week in Israel"?	yesh lekha gilayon aharon shel "This week in Israel"
What's on at the cinema tonight?	מָה מַצִּיגִים הָעֶרֶב בַּקּוֹלְנוֹעַ?	ma matzigim haerev bakolnoa
What's playing at the theatre?	מָה מַצִּיגִים בַּתֵּאַטְרוֹן?	ma matzigim bateatron
What sort of play is it?	אֵיזֶה מִן מַחֲזֶה זֶה?	eyze min mahaze ze
Who's it by?	מִי כָּתַב אוֹתוֹ?	mi katav oto
Where's that new film by . . . playing?	אֵיפֹה מַצִּיגִים אֶת הַסֶּרֶט הֶחָדָשׁ שֶׁל . . .?	eyfo matzigim et haseret hehadash shel

Can you recommend (a) . . . ?	אַתָּה יָכוֹל לְהַמְלִיץ עַל?	ata yakhol lehamlitz al
good film	סֶרֶט טוֹב	seret tov
comedy	קוֹמֶדְיָה	komedia
drama	דְּרָמָה	drama
musical	מַחֲזֶמֶר	maḥzemer
revue	רֶבְיָה	revia
thriller	סֶרֶט מֶתַח	seret metaḥ
Western	מַעֲרָבוֹן	maaravon
At what theatre is that new play by . . . showing?	אֵיפֹה מַצִּיגִים אֶת הַמַּחֲזֶה הֶחָדָשׁ שֶׁל ? . . .	eyfo matzigim et hamaḥaze heḥadash shel
Who's in it?	מִי הַשַּׂחְקָנִים?	mi hasaḥkanim
Who's playing the lead?	מִי מְשַׂחֵק בַּתַּפְקִיד הָרָאשִׁי?	mi mesaḥek batafkid harashi
Who's the director?	מִי הַבַּמַּאי?	mi habamay
What time does it begin?	בְּאֵיזֶה שָׁעָה הַהַתְחָלָה?	beeyze shaa hahathala
What time does the show end?	בְּאֵיזֶה שָׁעָה נִגְמֶרֶת הַהַצָּגָה?	beeyze shaa nigmeret hahatzaga
What time does the first evening performance start?	מָתַי מַתְחִילָה הַהַצָּגָה הָרִאשׁוֹנָה?	matay mathila hahatzaga harishona
Are there any tickets for tonight?	יֵשׁ עוֹד כַּרְטִיסִים הָעֶרֶב?	yesh od kartisim haerev
I want to reserve two tickets for the show on Saturday evening.	אֲנִי רוֹצֶה לְהַזְמִין שְׁנֵי כַּרְטִיסִים לְמוֹצָאֵי שַׁבָּת.	ani rotze lehazmin sheney kartisim lemotzaey shabat
Can I have a ticket for the matinee on Tuesday?	אֶפְשָׁר לְהַשִּׂיג כַּרְטִיס לְהַצָּגַת בּוֹקֶר בְּיוֹם חֲמִישִׁי?	efshar lehasig kartis lehatzagat boker beyom ḥamishi
I want a seat in the stalls (orchestra).	הָיִיתִי רוֹצֶה מָקוֹם בַּתָּא.	hayiti rotze makom bata
Not too far back.	לֹא יוֹתֵר מִדַּי רָחוֹק, בְּבַקָּשָׁה.	lo yoter miday raḥok, bevakasha

Somewhere in the middle.	אֲבַקֵּשׁ מָקוֹם בָּאֶמְצַע.	avakesh makom baemtza
May I have a programme, please?	אֶפְשָׁר לְקַבֵּל תָּכְנִיָּה, בְּבַקָּשָׁה?	efshar lekabel tokhniya, bevakasha
Can I check this coat?	אֶפְשָׁר לִמְסוֹר אֶת הַמְּעִיל?	efshar limsor et hameil
Here's my ticket.	הִנֵּה הַכַּרְטִיס שֶׁלִּי.	hine hakartis sheli

Opera—Ballet—Concert

Where's the opera house?	אֵיפֹה בֵּית הָאוֹפֵּרָה?	eyfo bet haopera
Where's the concert hall?	אֵיפֹה אוּלָם הַקּוֹנְצֵרְטִים?	eyfo ulam hakontzertim
What's on at the opera tonight?	מָה מַצִּיגִים הָעֶרֶב בָּאוֹפֵּרָה?	ma matzigim haerev baopera
Who's singing?	מִי הַזַּמָּר?	mi hazamar
Who's dancing?	מִי הָרַקְדָנִית?	mi harakdanit
What time does the programme start?	מָתַי הַהַתְחָלָה?	matay hahathala
What orchestra is playing?	אֵיזֶה תִּזְמוֹרֶת מְנַגֶּנֶת?	eyze tizmoret menagenet
What are they playing?	מָה הֵם מְנַגְּנִים?	ma hem menagnim
Who's the conductor?	מִי הַמְנַצֵּחַ?	mi hamenatzeah

Possible answers

מִצְטַעֵר, הַכַּרְטִיסִים אָזְלוּ.	I'm sorry, we're sold out.
נִשְׁאֲרוּ רַק מְקוֹמוֹת אֲחָדִים בַּיָּצִיעַ.	There are only a few seats in the balcony (circle).
אֶפְשָׁר לִרְאוֹת אֶת הַכַּרְטִיס?	May I see your ticket?
זֶה הַמָּקוֹם שֶׁלְּךָ.	This is your seat.

RELAXING

Night clubs

Night clubs are pretty much the same the world over—particularly when it comes to inflated prices. You can expect to pay a cover charge. Your drinks will be expensive. The girls sitting around aren't there because they like the decor.

There are some reasonably-priced places that provide good entertainment, so ask around. But find out the prices before you order—and allow for the various surcharges.

For most night clubs, jacket and tie are sufficient.

Can you recommend a good night club?	תּוּכַל לְהַמְלִיץ עַל מוֹעֲדוֹן לַיְלָה?	tukhal lehamlitz al moadon layla
Is there a floor show?	יֵשׁ שָׁם הוֹפָעָה?	yesh sham hofaa
What time does the floor show start?	מָתַי מַתְחִילָה הַהוֹפָעָה?	matay mathila hahofaa
Is evening dress necessary?	הַאִם תִּלְבּוֹשֶׁת עֶרֶב הֶכְרֵחִית?	haim tilboshet erev hekhrehit

And once inside . . .

A table for two, please.	שֻׁלְחָן לִשְׁנַיִם, בְּבַקָּשָׁה.	shulhan lishnayim, bevakasha
My name's . . . I reserved a table for four.	שְׁמִי.... הִזְמַנְתִּי שֻׁלְחָן לְאַרְבָּעָה.	shemi . . . , hizmanti makom learbaa
I telephoned you earlier.	דִּבַּרְתִּי אִתְּכֶם בְּטֶלֶפוֹן.	dibarti itkhem betelefon
We haven't got a reservation.	לֹא הִזְמַנּוּ מָקוֹם.	lo hizmannu makom

Dancing

Where can we go dancing?	לְאָן אֶפְשָׁר לָלֶכֶת לִרְקוֹד?	lean efshar lalekhet lirkod
Is there a discotheque anywhere here?	יֵשׁ דִּסְקוֹטֶק בַּסְּבִיבָה?	yesh diskotek baseviva
There's a ball at the . . .	יֵשׁ נֶשֶׁף רִקּוּדִים בְּ...	yesh neshef rikudim be
Would you like to dance?	אַתְּ מוּכָנָה לִרְקוֹד?	at mukhana lirkod
May I have this dance?	אֶפְשָׁר לְהַזְמִין אוֹתָךְ לְרִקּוּד זֶה?	efshar lehazmin otakh lerikud ze

Do you happen to play . . . ?

On rainy days, this page may solve your problems.

Do you happen to play chess?	אַתָּה מְשַׂחֵק שַׁח?	ata mesaḥek shaḥ
I'm afraid I don't.	לֹא אֵינֶנִּי מְשַׂחֵק.	lo, eyneni mesaḥek
No, but I'll give you a game of draughts (checkers).	לֹא, אֲבָל אֲנִי מוּכָן לְשַׂחֵק אִתְּךָ דַּמְקָה.	lo, aval ani mukhan lesaḥek itkha damka
king	מֶלֶךְ	melekh
queen	מַלְכָּה	malka
castle (rook)	צְרִיחַ	tzeriaḥ
bishop	רָץ	ratz
knight	סוּס	sus
pawn	חַיָל	ḥayal
Do you play cards?	אַתָּה מְשַׂחֵק קְלָפִים?	ata mesaḥek kelafim
ace	אַס	as
king	מֶלֶךְ	melekh
queen	מַלְכָּה	malka
jack	וַלֶט	valet
joker	ג׳וֹקֶר	joker

RELAXING

Spades	פִּיק	pik
Hearts	לֵב	lev
Diamonds	קָרוֹ	karo
Clubs	תִּלְתָּן	tiltan

Israel has no casinos. Gambling is against the law, and all money games are forbidden. But there's a national lottery and picking the soccer winners (guessing the weekly results) is a popular and sometimes rewarding pastime.

Oriental chess

A very popular game in Israel is oriental chess or backgammon, called *sheshbesh* in Hebrew. Shown below is the backgammon board. The game is played with dice. The winner is the one who first has all his checkers on the opposite side.

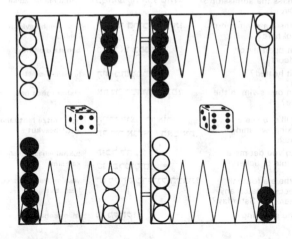

Sport

Football (soccer), basketball, tennis, fishing and swimming are the most popular sports. All sports are amateur. Winter sports are actually unknown (except for some skiing in Mount Hermon). Underwater fishing has recently been introduced and is rapidly increasing in popularity. Israel is an excellent place for all water sports.

Where's the nearest golf course?	אֵיפֹה מְשַׂחֲקִים כָּאן גּוֹלְף?	eyfo mesahakim kan golf
Can we hire (rent) clubs?	אֶפְשָׁר לִשְׂכּוֹר מַקְלוֹת גּוֹלְף?	efshar liskor maklot golf
Where are the tennis courts?	אֵיפֹה מִגְרָשׁ טֶנִיס?	eyfo migrash tenis
Can I hire rackets?	אֶפְשָׁר לִשְׂכּוֹר רָקֶטָה?	efshar liskor raketa
What's the charge per . . . ?	מַה הַתַּשְׁלוּם...?	ma hatashlum
day/round/hour	לְיוֹם / לְמִשְׂחָק / לְשָׁעָה	leyom/lemishak/leshaa
What's the admission charge?	כַּמָּה עוֹלָה הַכְּנִיסָה?	kama ola hakenisa
Is there a swimming pool here?	יֵשׁ כָּאן בְּרֵיכַת שְׂחִיָּה?	yesh kan bereykhat sehiya
Is it open-air or indoors?	בַּחוּץ אוֹ בִּפְנִים?	bahutz o bifnim
Is it heated?	הִיא מְחוּמֶּמֶת?	hi mehumemet
Can one swim in the lake?	אֶפְשָׁר לִשְׂחוֹת בַּאֲגַם?	efshar lishot baagam
I'd like to see a boxing/wrestling match.	הָיִיתִי רוֹצֶה לִרְאוֹת תַּחֲרוּת אִגְרוּף / הֵאָבְקוּת.	hayiti rotze lirot taharut igruf/heavkut
Can you get me a couple of tickets?	תּוּכַל לְהַשִּׂיג לִי שְׁנֵי כַּרְטִיסִים?	tukhal lehasig li sheney kartisim
Is there a football (soccer) match anywhere this Saturday?	יֵשׁ מִשְׂחַק כַּדּוּרֶגֶל הַשַּׁבָּת?	yesh mishak kaduregel hashabat
Who's playing?	מִי מְשַׂחֵק?	mi mesahek

Is there any good fishing around here?	אֶפְשָׁר לָדוּג פֹּה?	efshar ladug po
Do I need a permit?	דָּרוּשׁ רִשָׁיוֹן?	darush rishayon
Where can I get one?	אֵיפֹה מַשִׂיגִים רִשָׁיוֹן?	eyfo masigim rishayon
Where can I see a basketball game?	אֵיפֹה אֶפְשָׁר לִרְאוֹת מִשְׂחַק כַּדוּרְסַל?	eyfo efshar lirot mishak kadursal
Is there a volleyball game Saturday?	יֵשׁ מִשְׂחַק כַּדוּרְעָף בְּשַׁבָּת?	yesh mishak keduraf beshabat
Do they have a handball field?	יֵשׁ מִגְרָשׁ לְכַדוּרְיָד?	yesh migrash lekaduryad
Do you have a ping-pong championship?	יֵשׁ לָכֶם אֲלִיפוּת טֶנִיס שֻׁלְחָן?	yesh lakhem alifut tenis shulhan

On the beach

What's the beach like—sandy, shingle, rocky?	אֵיךְ הַחוֹף – חוֹלִי, עם אֲבָנִים, סַלְעִי?	ekh hahof—holi, im avanim, sali
Is it safe for swimming?	מוּתָּר כָּאן לִשְׂחוֹת?	mutar kan lishot
Is there a lifeguard?	יֵשׁ מַצִּיל?	yesh matzil
Is it safe for children?	הַיָּם בָּטוּחַ לִילָדִים?	hayam batuah liyeladim
It's very calm.	הַיָּם מְאֹד שָׁקֵט.	hayam meod shaket
Are there any dangerous currents?	יֵשׁ זְרָמִים מְסוּכָּנִים?	yesh zeramim mesukanim
What time is high tide?	מָתַי הַגֵּאוּת?	matay hageut
What time is low tide?	מָתַי הַשֶּׁפֶל?	matay hashefel
The water is warm/ cold.	הַמַּיִם חַמִּים / קָרִים.	hamayim hamim/karim
I want to hire . . .	אֲנִי רוֹצֶה לִשְׂכּוֹר . . .	ani rotze liskor
an air mattress	מִזְרוֹן אֲוִיר	mizron avir
a bathing hut	תָּא / קַבִּינָה	ta/kabina
a deck chair	כִּסֵּא נוֹחַ	kise noah

skin-diving equipment	צִיּוּד צְלִילָה	tsiyud tzelila
a sunshade	שִׁמְשִׁיָּה	shimshiya
a surf board	חֲסָקָה	hasaka
a tent	אֹהֶל	ohel
some water skis	מִגְלְשֵׁי מַיִם	migleshey mayim
Where can I rent . . . ?	אֵיפֹה אֶפְשָׁר לִשְׂכֹּר . . . ?	eyfo efshar liskor
a canoe	סִירָה	sira
a rowing boat	סִירַת מְשׁוֹטִים	sirat meshotim
a motor boat	סִירַת מָנוֹעַ	sirat manoa
a sailing boat	סִירַת מִפְרָשִׂים	sirat mifrasim
What's the charge per hour?	מַה הַתַּשְׁלוּם לְשָׁעָה?	ma hatashlum leshaa

RELAXING

| חוֹף פְּרָטִי | הָרְחִיצָה אֲסוּרָה |
| PRIVATE BEACH | NO BATHING |

Obviously, not the place for us. Let's move on.

Camping—Countryside

Thanks to its special climate (nine sunny months) Israel is a favourable country for camping. There are numerous camping sites, all of them with excellent facilities: shower stalls and washrooms, electricity, camp restaurants, bus connections, etc. All camping sites are under the official control of the Israel Camping Union.

If you want to camp on private land, get permission from the owner first.

Can we camp here?	מוּתָּר לַעֲשׂוֹת פֹּה קֶמְפִּינְג?	mutar laasot po camping
Where can one camp for the night?	אֵיפֹה אֶפְשָׁר לַעֲשׂוֹת קֶמְפִּינְג לַיְלָה אֶחָד?	eyfo efshar laasot camping lelayla ehad
Is there a camping site near here?	יֵשׁ חַנְיוֹן בַּסְּבִיבָה?	yesh hanyon baseviva
Is there drinking water?	יֵשׁ פֹּה מֵי שְׁתִיָּה?	yesh po mey shetiya
Are there shopping facilities on the site?	אֶפְשָׁר כָּאן לִקְנוֹת מַשֶּׁהוּ?	efshar kan liknot mashehu
Are there . . . ?	יֵשׁ כָּאן...?	yesh kan
baths	סִדּוּרֵי רַחֲצָה	sidurey rahatza
showers	מִקְלָחוֹת	miklahot
toilets	בָּתֵּי שִׁמּוּשׁ	batey shimush
What's the charge . . . ?	מָה הַתַּשְׁלוּם...?	ma hatashlum
per day	לְיוֹם	leyom
per person	לְאָדָם אֶחָד	leadam ehad
for a car	לִמְכוֹנִית	limekhonit
for a tent	לְאֹהֶל	leohel
Is there a youth hostel anywhere near here?	יֵשׁ אַכְסַנְיַת נֹעַר בַּסְּבִיבָה?	yesh akhsanyat noar baseviva
Do you know anyone who can put us up for the night?	אַתָּה מַכִּיר מִישֶׁהוּ שֶׁיּוּכַל לְאַכְסֵן אוֹתָנוּ הַלַּיְלָה?	ata makir mishehu sheyukhal leakhsen otanu halayla

FOR CAMPING EQUIPMENT, see page 106

CAMPING – COUNTRYSIDE

	אסור לעשות קמפינג CAMPING PROHIBITED	

How far is it to . . . ?	?...מַה הַמֶּרְחָק לְ	ma hamerhak le
How far is the next village?	?מַה הַמֶּרְחָק לַיִּשּׁוּב הַקָּרוֹב	ma hamerhak layishuv hakarov
Are we on the right road for . . . ?	?...זוֹהִי הַדֶּרֶךְ לְ	zohi haderekh le
Where does this road lead to?	?לְאָן מוֹבִילָה דֶּרֶךְ זֹאת	lean movila derekh zot
Can you show us where we are on the map?	תּוּכַל לְהַרְאוֹת עַל ?הַמַּפָּה אֵיפֹה אָנוּ נִמְצָאִים	tukhal leharot al hamapa eyfo anu nimtzaim

Landmarks

airfield	שְׂדֵה תְּעוּפָה	sedey teufa
bridge	גֶּשֶׁר	gesher
building	בִּנְיָן	binyan
canal	תְּעָלָה	teala
church	כְּנֵסִיָּה	kenesiya
cliff	צוּק	tzuk
copse	חֻרְשָׁה	hursha
desert	מִדְבָּר	midbar
excavations	חֲפִירוֹת	hafirot
farm	מֶשֶׁק	meshek
ferry	מַעֲבֹּרֶת	maaboret
field	שָׂדֶה	sade
footpath	שְׁבִיל	shevil
hamlet	כְּפָר	kefar
hill	גִּבְעָה	giva
house	בַּיִת	bayit
inn	אַכְסַנְיָה	akhsanya
kibbutz	קִבּוּץ	kibutz

lake	אֲגַם	agam
mountain	הַר	har
mountain range	רֶכֶס	rekhes
orange grove	פַּרְדֵּס	pardes
path	דֶּרֶךְ	derekh
peak	פִּסְגָּה	pisga
plain	מִישׁוֹר	mishor
plantation	מַטָּע	mata
pool	בְּרֵיכַת שְׂחִיָּה	bereykhat sehiya
river	נָהָר	nahar
road	כְּבִישׁ	kevish
sand dunes	חוֹלוֹת	holot
seashore	חוֹף הַיָּם	hof hayam
spring	מַעְיָן	maayan
tel	תֵּל	tel
tower	מִגְדָּל	migdal
tree	עֵץ	etz
valley	עֵמֶק	emek
village	עֲיָרָה	ayara
vineyard	כֶּרֶם	kerem
wadi	וָדִי	wadi
water	מַיִם	mayim
waterfall	מַפַּל מַיִם	mapal mayim
well	בְּאֵר	beer
wood	יַעַר	yaar
What's the name of this place?	אֵיךְ קוֹרְאִים לַמָּקוֹם הַזֶּה?	ekh korim lamakom haze
How high is that mountain?	מַה גֹּבַהּ הָהָר הַזֶּה?	ma gova hahar haze

... and if you're tired of walking, you can always try hitch-hiking—though you may have to wait a long time for a lift.

| Can you give me a lift to . . . ? | תּוּכַל לָתֵת לִי טְרֶמְפ לְ...? | tukhal latet li tremp le |

Making friends

Introductions

Here are a few phrases to get you started.

How do you do? How are you?	מַה שְׁלוֹמְךָ?	ma shelomkha
Very well, thank you.	טוֹב מְאֹד, תּוֹדָה.	tov meod, toda
How's it going?	מַה נִשְׁמַע?	ma nishma
Fine thanks. And you?	יָפֶה, תּוֹדָה וְאֶצְלְךָ?	yafe, toda, veetzlekha
May I introduce Miss ...	נָא לְהַכִּיר אֶת הַגְּבֶרֶת ...	na lehakir et hageveret
I'd like you to meet a friend of mine.	תַּכִּיר, בְּבַקָשָׁה, יְדִיד שֶׁלִי.	takir, bevakasha, yedid sheli
Arieh, this is ...	אַרְיֵה, תַּכִּיר בְּבַקָשָׁה אֶת ...	Arye, takir bevakasha et
My name's ...	שְׁמִי ...	shemi
Delighted to meet you.	אֲנִי שָׂמֵחַ לְהַכִּיר אוֹתְךָ.	ani sameah lehakir otkha
Glad to know you.	נָעִים מְאֹד.	naim meod

Follow-up

How long have you been here?	כַּמָּה זְמָן אַתָה בָּאָרֶץ?	kama zeman ata baaretz
We've been here a week.	אָנוּ פֹּה שָׁבוּעַ.	anu po shavua
Is this your first visit?	זֶה בִּקוּרְךָ הָרִאשׁוֹן?	ze bikurkha harishon
No, we came here last year.	לֹא, הָיִינוּ כָּאן בַּשָׁנָה שֶׁעָבְרָה.	lo, hayinu kan bashana sheavra
Are you enjoying your stay?	אַתָה נֶהֱנֶה כָּאן?	ata nehne kan

Yes, I like . . . very much.	כֵּן, שָׂמַחְתִּי מְאֹד לִרְאוֹת אֶת...	ken, samaḥti meod lirot et
I'm with . . .	אֲנִי כָּאן עִם...	ani kan im
my wife	אִשְׁתִּי	ishti
my family	מִשְׁפַּחְתִּי	mishpaḥti
my parents	הוֹרַי	horay
some friends	כַּמָּה חֲבֵרִים	kama ḥaverim
Where do you come from?	מִנַּיִן אַתָּה?	minain ata
What part of . . . do you come from?	מֵאֵיזֶה חֵלֶק שֶׁל.... אַתָּה בָּא?	meeyze ḥelek shel ata ba
I'm from . . .	אֲנִי בָּא מִ...	ani ba me
Do you live here?	אַתָּה גָּר כָּאן?	ata gar kan
I'm a student.	אֲנִי סְטוּדֶנְט.	ani student
What are you studying?	מָה אַתָּה לוֹמֵד?	ma ata lomed
We're here on holiday.	אָנוּ כָּאן בְּחוּפְשָׁה.	anu kan beḥufsha
I'm here on a business trip.	אֲנִי כָּאן לְרֶגֶל עֲסָקִים.	ani kan leregel asakim
What kind of business are you in?	בַּמֶּה אַתָּה עוֹסֵק?	bame ata osek
I hope we'll see you again soon.	אֲנִי מְקַוֶּה שֶׁנִּתְרָאֶה בְּקָרוֹב.	ani mekave shenitrae bekarov
See you later/See you tomorrow.	לְהִתְרָאוֹת / לְהִתְרָאוֹת מָחָר.	lehitraot/lehitraot maḥar
I'm sure we'll run into each other again some time.	אֲנִי בָּטוּחַ שֶׁנִּתְרָאֶה אֵי־פַּעַם.	ani batuaḥ shenitrae ey-paam

The weather

They talk about the weather just as much in Israel as the British are supposed to do. So . . .

What a lovely day!	אֵיזֶה יוֹם יָפֶה!	eyze yom yafe
What awful weather!	מֶזֶג אֲוִיר אָיוֹם!	mezeg avir ayom
Isn't it cold today?	אֵיזֶה קוֹר הַיּוֹם!	eyze kor hayom
Isn't it hot today?	אֵיזֶה חוֹם הַיּוֹם!	eyze ḥom hayom
Is it usually as warm as this?	הַאִם תָּמִיד כָּל כָּךְ חַם?	haim tamid kol kakh ḥam
What's the temperature outside?	כַּמָּה מַעֲלוֹת הַיּוֹם?	kama maalot hayom
The wind is very strong.	הָרוּחַ חֲזָקָה מְאֹד.	haruaḥ ḥazaka meod

Invitations

My wife and I would like you to dine with us on . . .	אִשְׁתִּי וַאֲנִי מַזְמִינִים אֶתְכֶם לַאֲרוּחַת עֶרֶב בְּיוֹם...	ishti vaani mazminim etkhem laaruḥat erev beyom
Can you come to dinner tomorrow night?	תּוּכַל לָבוֹא לַאֲרוּחַת עֶרֶב מָחָר?	tukhal lavo laaruḥat erev maḥar
We're giving a small party tomorrow night. I do hope you can come.	אָנוּ עוֹרְכִים מְסִיבָּה קְטַנָּה מָחָר בָּעֶרֶב, אֲנִי מְקַוֶּה שֶׁתּוּכְלוּ לָבוֹא.	anu orkhim mesiba ketana mahar baerev; ani mekave shetukhlu lavo
Can you come round for cocktails this evening?	תּוּכְלוּ לָבוֹא אֵלֵינוּ לְקוֹקְטֵייל הָעֶרֶב?	tukhlu lavo eleynu lecocktail haerev
There's a party. Are you coming?	יֵשׁ מְסִיבָּה; אַת בָּאָה?	yesh mesiba; at baa
That's very kind of you.	נֶחְמָד מְאֹד מִצִּדְךָ.	neḥmad meod mitzidkha
Great, I'd love to come.	יוֹפִי, אֶשְׂמַח לָבוֹא.	yofi, esmaḥ lavo

FOR TEMPERATURE, see page 183

What time shall we come?	בְּאֵיזֶה שָׁעָה לָבוֹא?	beeyze shaa lavo
May I bring a friend?	מוּתָּר לְהָבִיא חָבֵר / חֲבֵרָה?	mutar lehavi haver/ havera
I'm afraid we've got to go now.	צַר לִי שֶׁעָלֵינוּ לַעֲזוֹב כָּעֵת.	tzar li shealeynu laazov kaet
Next time you must come to visit us.	בַּפַּעַם הַבָּאָה אַתֶּם חַיָּבִים לְבַקֵּר אֶצְלֵנוּ.	bapaam habaa atem hayavim levaker etzleynu
Thank you very much for an enjoyable evening.	תּוֹדָה רַבָּה עַל הָעֶרֶב הַנֶּחְמָד.	toda raba al haerev hanehmad
Thanks for the party. It was great.	תּוֹדָה עַל הַמְּסִיבָּה; הָיָה יוֹצֵא מִן הַכְּלָל.	toda al hamesiba; haya yotze min haklal

Dating

Would you like a cigarette?	אַתְּ מְעַשֶּׁנֶת?	at meashenet
Have you got a light, please?	אֶפְשָׁר לְבַקֵּשׁ אֵשׁ?	efshar levakesh esh
Can I get you a drink?	אֶפְשָׁר לְהַצִּיעַ לָךְ מַשֶּׁהוּ לִשְׁתּוֹת?	efshar lehatzia lakh mashehu lishtot
Excuse me, could you help me, please?	סְלִיחָה, תּוּכְלִי לַעֲזוֹר לִי, בְּבַקָּשָׁה?	seliha, tukhli laazor li, bevakasha
I'm lost. Can you show me the way to . . .?	טָעִיתִי בַּדֶּרֶךְ, תּוּכְלִי לְהַרְאוֹת לִי אֶת הַדֶּרֶךְ לְ...?	taiti baderekh, tukhli leharot li et haderekh le
You've dropped your handkerchief . . .	הַמִּטְפַּחַת שֶׁלָּךְ נָפְלָה.	hamitpahat shelakh nafla
Are you waiting for someone?	אַתְּ מְחַכָּה לְמִישֶׁהוּ?	at mehaka lemishehu
Are you free this evening?	אַתְּ פְּנוּיָה הָעֶרֶב?	at penuya haerev
Would you like to come out with me tonight?	אַתְּ מוּכָנָה לָצֵאת אִתִּי הָעֶרֶב?	at mukhana latzet iti haerev

Would you like to go dancing?	אַת רוֹצָה לָלֶכֶת לִרְקוֹד?	at rotza lalekhet lirkod
Shall we go to the cinema (movies)?	אַת רוֹצָה לָלֶכֶת לְסֶרֶט?	at rotza lalekhet leseret
Would you like to go for a drive?	אַת רוֹצָה לְטַיֵּל בַּמְכוֹנִית?	at rotza letayel bamekhonit
I'd love to, thank you.	אֶשְׂמַח מְאֹד, תּוֹדָה.	esmaḥ meod, toda
Where shall we meet?	הֵיכָן נִפָּגֵשׁ?	heykhan nipagesh
I'll pick you up at your hotel.	אָבוֹא לָקַחַת אוֹתָךְ מִן הַמָּלוֹן.	avo lakaḥat otakh min hamalon
I'll call for you at eight.	אָבוֹא לָקַחַת אוֹתָךְ בִּשְׁמוֹנֶה בָּעֶרֶב.	avo lakaḥat otakh bishmone baerev
May I take you home?	אֶפְשָׁר לְלַווֹת אוֹתָךְ הַבַּיְתָה?	efshar lelavot otakh habayta
Can I see you again tomorrow?	נוּכַל לְהִתְרָאוֹת מָחָר?	nukhal lehitraot maḥar
Thank you, it's been a wonderful evening.	תּוֹדָה, הָיָה עֶרֶב נִפְלָא.	toda, haya erev nifla
I've enjoyed myself tremendously.	נֶהֱנֵיתִי מְאֹד.	nehneyti meod
What's your telephone number?	מַה מִסְפַּר הַטֶּלֶפוֹן שֶׁלָּךְ?	ma mispar hatelefon shelakh
Do you live with your family?	אַת גָּרָה עִם מִשְׁפַּחְתֵּךְ?	at gara im mishpaḥtekh
Do you live alone?	אַת גָּרָה לְבַד?	at gara levad
What time is your last bus?	מָתַי הָאוֹטוֹבּוּס הָאַחֲרוֹן?	matay haotobus haaharon

Shopping guide

This shopping guide is designed to help you find what you want with ease, accuracy and speed. It features:

1. a list of all major shops, stores and services;
2. some general expressions required when shopping to allow you to be specific and selective;
3. full details of the shops and services most likely to concern you. Here you will find advice, alphabetical lists of items and conversion charts listed under the headings below.

	Main items	Page
Bookshop	books, magazines, newspapers, stationery	104
Camping	camping supplies	106
Chemist's (pharmacy)	medicine, first-aid, cosmetics, toilet articles	108
Clothing	clothes, shoes, accessories	112
Electrical appliances	radios, tape recorders, shavers, records	119
Hairdresser's	barber's, ladies' hairdresser, beauty salon	121
Jeweller's	jewellery, watches, watch repairs	123
Laundry—Dry cleaning	usual facilities	126
Photography	cameras, accessories, films, developing	127
Provisions	this is confined to basic items required for picnics	129
Souvenirs	souvenirs, gifts, fancy goods	131
Tobacconist's	smoker's requisites	132

LISTED BY
THE MINISTRY
OF TOURISM

Watch out for this sign, displayed by shops and services catering for tourists. It is issued by Israel's Ministry of Tourism, and means "recommended for reliability and quality".

From Sunday to Thursday, shops in Israel usually open at 8.30 a.m. and close at 7 p.m. They all close for lunch from 1.30 to 3.30 p.m. On Fridays and days preceding Jewish holidays, they close at about 4 p.m. (two hours before sunset).

Israel has kept many traditional Oriental customs, one of which is the art of bargaining. In big shops prices are fixed, but in the bazaars (*shuk*) and in small shops it's advisable to bargain.

Where's the nearest . . . ?	אֵיפֹה הַ... הַקָּרוֹב בְּיוֹתֵר?	eyfo ha . . . hakarov beyoter
antique shop	חֲנוּת עַתִּיקוֹת	ḥanut atikot
art gallery	גַּלֶרְיָה לְאָמָנוּת	galeria leomanut
bakery	מַאֲפִיָּה	maafiya
bank	בַּנְק	bank
barber shop	מִסְפָּרָה	mispara
beauty parlour	מָכוֹן לְיוֹפִי	makhon leyofi
bookshop	חֲנוּת סְפָרִים	ḥanut sefarim
butcher	אִטְלִיז	itliz
candy store	חֲנוּת מַמְתַּקִים	ḥanut mamtakim
chemist	בֵּית־מִרְקַחַת	bet mirkaḥat
clothing store	חֲנוּת הַלְבָּשָׁה	ḥanut halbasha
confectioner	מִגְדָּנִיָּה	migdaniya
dairy shop	חֲנוּת לְמוּצְרֵי חָלָב	ḥanut lemutzrey ḥalav
delicatessen	מַעֲדָנִים	maadanim
dentist	רוֹפֵא שִׁנַּיִם	rofe shinayim
department store	חֲנוּת כָּל־בּוֹ	ḥanut kol-bo
doctor	רוֹפֵא	rofe
dressmaker	תּוֹפֶרֶת	toferet
drugstore	בֵּית־מִרְקַחַת	bet mirkaḥat
dry cleaner	נִקּוּי יָבֵשׁ	nikuy yavesh
fish monger	חֲנוּת דָּגִים	ḥanut dagim
florist	חֲנוּת פְּרָחִים	ḥanut peraḥim

furrier	פַּרְווֹת	parvot
greengrocer	חֲנוּת יְרָקוֹת	ḥanut yerakot
grocery	מַכֹּלֶת	makolet
hairdresser	סַפָּר	sapar
hardware store	חֲנוּת לַחוֹמְרֵי בַּרְזֶל	ḥanut leḥomrey barzel
hat shop	כּוֹבָעִים	kovaim
hospital	בֵּית חוֹלִים	bet ḥolim
jeweller	תַכְשִׁיטִים	takhshitim
laundry	מַכְבֵּסָה	makhbesa
liquor store	חֲנוּת לְמַשְׁקָאוֹת	ḥanut lemashkaot
market	שׁוּק	shuk
newsagent	סוֹכְנוּת עִתּוֹנִים	sokhnut itonim
newsstand	דּוּכַן עִתּוֹנִים	dukhan itonim
optician	אוֹפְּתִיקָאי	optikay
pastry shop	קוֹנְדִיטוֹרְיָה	konditorya
pharmacy	בֵּית מִרְקַחַת	bet mirkaḥat
photographer	צַלָם	tzalam
photo shop	חֲנוּת צִילוּם	ḥanut tzilum
police station	תַחֲנַת מִשְׁטָרָה	taḥanat mishtara
post office	דּוֹאַר	doar
shoemaker (repairs)	סַנְדְּלָר	sandelar
shoe shop	חֲנוּת נַעֲלַיִם	ḥanut naalayim
souvenir shop	חֲנוּת לְמַזְכָּרוֹת	ḥanut lemazkarot
sporting goods shop	חֲנוּת סְפּוֹרְט	ḥanut sport
stationer	חֲנוּת לְמַכְשִׁירֵי כְּתִיבָה	ḥanut lemakhshirey ketiva
supermarket	סוּפֶּרְסָל	supersal
tailor	חַיָּט	ḥayat
tobacconist	חֲנוּת לְסִיגַרְיוֹת	ḥanut lesigariyot
toy shop	חֲנוּת צַעֲצוּעִים	ḥanut tzaatzuim
travel agent	מִשְׂרַד נְסִיעוֹת	misrad nesiot
veterinarian	רוֹפֵא וֵטֵרִינָר	rofe veterinar
watchmaker	שָׁעָן	shaan
wine merchant	יֵינוֹת	yeynot

General expressions

Here are some expressions which will be useful to you when you're out shopping.

Where?

Where's a good . . . ?	אֵיפֹה אֶפְשָׁר לְהַשִּׂיג . . . טוֹב?	eyfo efshar lehasig . . . tov
Where's the nearest . . . ?	אֵיפֹה הַ . . . הַקָּרוֹב בְּיוֹתֵר?	eyfo ha . . . karov beyoter
Where can I find a . . . ?	אֵיפֹה אֲנִי מוֹצֵא . . . ?	eyfo ani motze
Where do they sell . . . ?	אֵיפֹה מוֹכְרִים . . . ?	eyfo mokherim
Can you recommend an inexpensive . . . ?	תּוּכַל לְהַמְלִיץ עַל . . . זוֹל?	tukhal lehamlitz al . . . zol
Where's the main shopping centre?	אֵיפֹה מֶרְכַּז הַקְּנִיּוֹת?	eyfo merkaz hakeniyot
How far is it from here?	מַה הַמֶּרְחָק מִכָּאן?	ma hamerhak mikan
How do I get there?	אֵיךְ אַגִּיעַ לְשָׁם?	ekh agia lesham

Service

Can you help me?	תּוּכְלִי לַעֲזוֹר לִי?	tukhli laazor li
I'm just looking around.	אֲנִי רַק מִסְתַּכֵּל.	ani rak mistakel
I want . . .	אֲנִי רוֹצֶה . . .	ani rotze
Can you show me some . . . ?	תּוּכְלִי לְהַרְאוֹת לִי כַּמָּה . . . ?	tukhli leharot li kama
Have you any . . . ?	יֵשׁ לָךְ . . . ?	yesh lakh

That one

Can you show me . . . ?	אֶפְשָׁר לִרְאוֹת . . . ?	efshar lirot
It's over there.	זֶה שָׁם.	ze sham

Defining the article

I want a . . . one.	אֲנִי רוֹצֶה אֶחָד...	ani rotze ehad
big	גָדוֹל	gadol
cheap	זוֹל	zol
dark	כֵּהֶה	kehe
good	טוֹב	tov
heavy	כָּבֵד	kaved
large	רָחָב	rahav
light (weight)	קַל	kal
light (colour)	בָּהִיר	bahir
rectangular	מַלְבֵּנִי	malbeni
round	עָגוֹל	agol
small	קָטָן	katan
square	מְרֻבָּע	meruba
I don't want anything too expensive.	שֶׁלֹּא יִהְיֶה יָקָר מִדַּי.	shelo ihye yakar miday

Preference

I prefer something of better quality.	אֲנִי רוֹצֶה מַשֶּׁהוּ יוֹתֵר טוֹב.	ani rotze mashehu yoter tov
Can you show me some more?	יֵשׁ עוֹד מַשֶּׁהוּ מִסּוּג זֶה?	yesh od mashehu misug ze
Haven't you anything . . . ?	יֵשׁ עוֹד מַשֶּׁהוּ יוֹתֵר...?	yesh od mashehu yoter
cheaper/better/ larger/smaller	זוֹל / טוֹב / רָחָב / קָטָן	zol/tov/rahav/katan

How much?

How much is this?	מַה הַמְּחִיר?	ma hamehir
I don't understand. Please write it down.	אֵינֶנִּי מֵבִין; תִּכְתֹּב אֶת זֶה, בְּבַקָּשָׁה.	eyneni mevin; tikhtov et ze, bevakasha
I don't want to spend more than 50 pounds.	אֵינֶנִּי רוֹצֶה לְהוֹצִיא יוֹתֵר מֵחֲמִשִּׁים לִירוֹת.	eyneni rotze lehotzi yoter mehamishim lirot

FOR COLOURS, see page 113

SHOPPING GUIDE

Decision

That's just what I want.	זֶה בְּדִיוּק מַה שֶׁאֲנִי רוֹצֶה.	ze bediyuk ma sheani rotze
No, I don't like it.	לֹא, זֶה לֹא מוֹצֵא חֵן בְּעֵינַי.	lo, ze lo motze ḥen beeynay
I'll take it.	אֲנִי לוֹקֵחַ אֶת זֶה.	ani lokeaḥ et ze

Ordering

Can you order it for me?	תּוּכַל לְהַזְמִין אֶת זֶה בִּשְׁבִילִי?	tukhal lehazmin et ze bishvili
How long will it take?	כַּמָּה זְמַן זֶה יִקַּח?	kama zeman ze ikaḥ

Delivery

I'll take it with me.	אֶקַּח אֶת זֶה אִתִּי.	ekaḥ et ze iti
Deliver it to the . . . hotel.	תִּשְׁלַח אֶת זֶה לְמָלוֹן . . .	tishlaḥ et ze lemalon
Please send it to this address.	אֲבַקֵּשׁ לִשְׁלוֹחַ אֶת זֶה לִכְתוֹבֶת זֹאת.	avakesh lishloaḥ et ze likhtovet zot
Will I have any difficulty with the customs?	יִהְיוּ לִי בְּעָיוֹת בַּמֶּכֶס?	ihyu beayot bamekhes

Paying

How much is it?	כַּמָּה זֶה עוֹלֶה?	kama ze ole
Can I pay by traveller's cheque?	אוּכַל לְשַׁלֵּם בְּהַמְחָאַת נוֹסְעִים?	ukhal leshalem behamḥaat nosim
Do you accept credit cards?	אַתֶּם מְקַבְּלִים כַּרְטִיסֵי אַשְׁרַאי?	atem mekabelim kartisey ashray
Haven't you made a mistake in the bill?	אֵין טָעוּת בְּחֶשְׁבּוֹן זֶה?	en taut beheshbon ze
Can I have a receipt, please?	אוּכַל לְקַבֵּל קַבָּלָה?	ukhal lekabel kabala

Anything else?

No, thanks, that's all.	לֹא תוֹדָה, זֶה הַכֹּל.	lo, toda, ze hakol
Yes, I want . . . / Show me . . .	כֵּן, אֲנִי רוֹצֶה . . . / תַּרְאֶה לִי . . .	ken, ani rotze . . . /tare li
Thank you. Good-bye.	תוֹדָה, לְהִתְרָאוֹת.	toda, lehitraot

Dissatisfied

Can you change this, please?	תּוּכַל לְהַחְלִיף אֶת זֶה, בְּבַקָּשָׁה?	tukhal lehahlif et ze, bevakasha
I want to return this.	אֲנִי רוֹצֶה לְהַחְזִיר אֶת זֶה.	ani rotze lehahzir et ze

Possible answers

אוּכַל לַעֲזוֹר לְךָ?	Can I help you?
בַּמֶּה אַתָּה מְעֻנְיָן? אֵיזֶה . . . ?	What . . . would you like?
צֶבַע / צוּרָה	colour/shape
טִיב / כַּמּוּת	quality/quantity
אֲנִי מִצְטַעֵר, אֵין לָנוּ.	I'm sorry, we haven't any.
לְהַזְמִין אֶת זֶה בִּשְׁבִילְךָ?	Shall we order it for you?
תִּקַּח אֶת זֶה אִתְּךָ, אוֹ נִשְׁלַח אֵלֶיךָ?	Will you take it with you or shall we send it?
זֶה עוֹלֶה . . . לִירוֹת.	That's . . . pounds, please.
אֵינֶנּוּ מְקַבְּלִים . . .	We don't accept . . .
כַּרְטִיסֵי אַשְׁרַאי	credit cards
הַמְחָאוֹת נוֹסְעִים	traveller's cheques
צֶ'קִים פְּרָטִיִּים	personal cheques

SHOPPING GUIDE

Bookshop—Stationer's—Newsstand

In Israel, bookshops and stationers may be combined or separate. Newspapers and magazines may be sold in bookshops, in kiosks or at the stationer's.

Where's the nearest . . . ?	אֵיפֹה . . . הַקָּרוֹב בְּיוֹתֵר ?	eyfo ha . . . karov beyoter
bookshop	חֲנוּת סְפָרִים	hanut sefarim
stationer's	חֲנוּת לְמַכְשִׁירֵי כְּתִיבָה	hanut lemakhshirey ketiva
newsstand	דּוּכַן עִתּוֹנִים	dukhan itonim
I want to buy a/an/ some . . .	אֲנִי רוֹצֶה לִקְנוֹת . . .	ani rotze liknot
address book	פִּנְקָס כְּתוֹבוֹת	pinkas ketovot
ball-point pen	עֵט כַּדּוּרִי	et kaduri
book	סֵפֶר	sefer
box of paints	קוּפְסַת צְבָעִים	kufsat tzevaim
carbon paper	נְיַר פֶּחָם	neyar peham
cellophane tape	נְיַר דֶּבֶק	neyar devek
crayons	עֶפְרוֹנוֹת צִיּוּר	efronot tziyur
dictionary	מִלּוֹן	milon
Hebrew-English	עִבְרִי־אַנְגְּלִי	ivri-angli
English-Hebrew	אַנְגְּלִי־עִבְרִי	angli-ivri
pocket dictionary	מִלּוֹן כִּיס	milon kis
drawing paper	נְיַר לְצִיּוּר	neyar letziyur
drawing pins	נְעָצִים	neatzim
elastic bands	גּוּמִיּוֹת	gumiyot
envelopes	מַעֲטָפוֹת	maatafot
eraser	מַחַק	mahak
fountain pen	עֵט נוֹבֵעַ	et novea
glue	דֶּבֶק	devek
grammar book	סֵפֶר דִּקְדּוּק	sefer dikduk
guide book	מַדְרִיךְ לְתַיָּרִים	madrikh letayarim
ink	דְּיוֹ	deyo
black/red/blue	שְׁחוֹרָה / אֲדוּמָה / כְּחוּלָה	shehora/aduma/kehula

labels	תָּוִיּוֹת	taviyot
magazine	עִתּוֹן מְצֻיָּר	iton metzuyar
map	מַפָּה	mapa
map of the town	מַפַּת הָעִיר	mapat hair
road map	מַפַּת דְּרָכִים	mapat derakhim
newspaper	עִתּוֹן	iton
American/English	אֲמֶרִיקָאִי / אַנְגְּלִי	amerikai/angli
notebook	פִּנְקָס	pinkas
note paper	נְיָר כְּתִיבָה	neyar ketiva
paperback	סֵפֶר כִּיס	sefer kis
paper napkins	מַפִּיּוֹת נְיָר	mapiyot neyar
paste	מִשְׁחַת דֶּבֶק	mishhat devek
pen	עֵט	et
pencil	עִפָּרוֹן	iparon
pencil sharpener	מְחַדֵּד	mehaded
postcards	גְּלוּיוֹת דּוֹאַר	geluyot doar
refill (for a pen)	מִלּוּי (לְעֵט)	miluy (leet)
rubber bands	סְרָטֵי גּוּמִי	sirtey gumi
ruler	סַרְגֵּל	sargel
sketching block	בְּלוֹק לְצִיּוּר	blok letziyur
stamps	בּוּלִים	bulim
string	חֶבֶל	hevel
thumb tacks	נְעָצִים	neatzim
tissue paper	נְיָר דַּק	neyar dak
typewriter ribbon	סֶרֶט לִמְכוֹנַת כְּתִיבָה	seret limkhonat ketiva
typing paper	נְיָר לִמְכוֹנַת כְּתִיבָה	neyar limkhonat ketiva
wrapping paper	נְיָר עֲטִיפָה	neyar atifa
writing pad	בְּלוֹק לִכְתִיבָה	blok likhtiva
Where's the guide-book section?	אֵיפֹה כָּאן הַמַּדְרִיכִים לְתַיָּרִים?	eyfo kan hamadrikhim letayarim
Where do you keep the English books?	אֵיפֹה כָּאן הַסְּפָרִים בְּאַנְגְּלִית?	eyfo kan hasefarim beanglit

Camping

I'd like a/an/some . . .	. . . אֲנִי רוֹצֶה לִקְנוֹת	ani rotze liknot
axe	גַּרְזֶן	garzen
bottle-opener	פּוֹתְחָן בַּקְבּוּקִים	pothan bakbukim
bucket	דְּלִי	deli
butane gas	גַּז	gaz
camp cot	מִטַּת שָׂדֶה	mitat sade
camping equipment	צִיּוּד לְקַמְפִּינְג	tziyud lecamping
can opener	פּוֹתְחָן קוּפְסָאוֹת	pothan kufsaot
candles	נֵרוֹת	nerot
chair	כִּסֵּא	kise
compass	מַצְפֵּן	matzpen
corkscrew	מַחְלֵץ לִפְקָקִים	mahletz lipkakim
deck chair	כִּסֵּא נוֹחַ	kise noah
first-aid kit	תִּיק עֶזְרָה רִאשׁוֹנָה	tik ezra rishona
flashlight	פָּנַס יָד	panas yad
frying pan	מַחֲבַת	mahavat
groundsheet	שְׂמִיכָה	semikha
hammer	פַּטִּישׁ	patish
hammock	עַרְסָל	arsal
ice-bag	שַׂקִּית לְקֶרַח	sakit lekerah
kerosine	נֵפְט	neft
kettle	קוּמְקוּם	kumkum
lamp	מְנוֹרָה	menora
lantern	פָּנַס	panas
matches	גַּפְרוּרִים	gafrurim
mattress	מִזְרוֹן	mizron
methylated spirits	סְפִּירְט	spirt
mosquito net	כִּלָּה נֶגֶד יַתּוּשִׁים	kila neged yatushim
paraffin	נֵפְט	neft
picnic case	צֵידָנִית	tzeydanit
pressure cooker	סִיר לַחַץ	sir lahatz

primus stove	פְּרִימוּס	primus
rope	חֶבֶל	ḥevel
rucksack	תַּרְמִיל־גַּב	tarmil-gav
saucepan	סִיר	sir
screwdriver	מַבְרֵג	mavreg
sheathknife	סַכִּין צוֹפִים	sakin tzofim
sleeping bag	שַׂק שֵׁנָה	sak sheyna
stove	תַּנּוּר חִמּוּם	tanur ḥimum
table	שֻׁלְחָן	shulḥan
tent	אֹהֶל	ohel
tent pegs	יְתֵדוֹת לָאֹהֶל	yetedot leohel
tent poles	מוֹטוֹת לָאֹהֶל	motot leohel
thermos flask (bottle)	תֶּרְמוֹס	termos
tin opener	פּוֹתְחָן קֻפְסָאוֹת	potḥan kufsaot
tongs	צְבָת	tzevat
torch	פָּנַס יָד	panas yad
vacuum flask	תֶּרְמוֹס	termos
water carrier	גֶּ׳רִיקָן	jerrycan

Crockery

cups	כּוֹסוֹת	kosot
food box	תֵּיבַת אוֹכֶל	tevat okhel
mugs	סְפָלִים	sefalim
plates	צַלָּחוֹת	tzalaḥot
saucers	תַּחְתִּיּוֹת	taḥtiyot

Cutlery

forks	מַזְלֵגוֹת	mazlegot
knives	סַכִּינִים	sakinim
spoons	כַּפּוֹת	kapot
teaspoons	כַּפִּיּוֹת	kapiyot
(made of) plastic	מִפְּלַסְטִיק	miplastik
(made of) stainless steel	מִפְּלָדָה לֹא־מַחְלִידָה	miplada lo-maḥlida

Chemist's (pharmacy)—Drugstore

Israeli chemists normally don't stock the great range of goods that you'll find in England or the U.S. In the window you'll see a notice telling you where the nearest all-night chemist is.

For reading ease, this section has been divided into two parts:
1. Pharmaceutical—medicine, first-aid, etc.
2. Toiletry—toilet articles, cosmetics.

General

Where's the nearest chemist?	אֵיפֹה בֵּית־הַמִּרְקַחַת הַקָּרוֹב בְּיוֹתֵר?	eyfo bet-hamirkaḥat hakarov beyoter
What time does the chemist open?	מָתַי פּוֹתְחִים אֶת בֵּית־ הַמִּרְקַחַת?	matay poteḥim et bet-hamirkaḥat
When does the chemist close?	מָתַי סוֹגְרִים אֶת בֵּית־הַמִּרְקַחַת?	matay sogerim et bet-hamirkaḥat

Part 1—Pharmaceutical

I want something for . . .	אֲנִי רוֹצֶה מַשֶּׁהוּ נֶגֶד ...	ani rotze mashehu neged
Can you recommend something for . . . ?	תּוּכַל לְהַצִּיעַ מַשֶּׁהוּ נֶגֶד ...	tukhal lehatzia mashehu neged
a cold/a cough	הִצְטַנְּנוּת / שִׁעוּל	hitztanenut/shiul
a hangover	כְּאֵב רֹאשׁ	keev rosh
sunburn	כְּוִיּוֹת שֶׁמֶשׁ	keviyot shemesh
travel sickness	מַחֲלַת נְסִיעָה	maḥalat nesia
Can you make up this prescription?	אֶפְשָׁר לְהָכִין בִּשְׁבִילִי אֶת הָרֶצֶפְּט הַזֶּה?	efshar lehakhin bishvili et haretzept haze
Shall I wait?	לְחַכּוֹת?	leḥakot
When shall I come back?	מָתַי לָבוֹא?	matay lavo

FOR DOCTORS, see page 162

Can I get it without a prescription?	אוּכַל לְקַבֵּל אֶת זֶה בְּלִי רֶצֶפְּט?	ukhal lekabel et ze beli retzept
Can I have a/an/some . . . ?	תֵּן לִי, בְּבַקָּשָׁה...	ten li, bevakasha
antiseptic cream	מִשְׁחָה אַנְטִיסֶפְּטִית	mishha antiseptit
bandage	תַחְבּוֹשֶׁת	tahboshet
gauze bandage	תַּחְבּוֹשֶׁת גָּזָה	tahboshet gaza
castor oil	שֶׁמֶן קִיק	shemen kik
contraceptives	תַּכְשִׁירֵי מְנִיעָה	takhshirey menia
corn plasters	פְּלַסְטֶרִים לְיַבָּלוֹת	plasterim leyabalot
cotton wool	צֶמֶר גֶּפֶן	tzemer gefen
cough lozenges	טַבְלֵטִים נֶגֶד שִׁעוּל	tabletim neged shiul
diabetic lozenges	טַבְלֵטִים לְסַכֶּרֶת	tabletim lesakeret
disinfectant	חֹמֶר חִיטוּי	homer hituy
ear drops	טִפּוֹת לָאָזְנַיִם	tipot leoznayim
eye drops	טִפּוֹת לָעֵינַיִם	tipot leeynayim
gargle	מֵי גִּרְגּוּר	mey girgur
gauze	גָּזָה	gaza
insect repellent	תַּכְשִׁיר נֶגֶד חֲרָקִים	takhshir neged harakim
iodine	יוֹד	yod
iron pills	גְּלוּלוֹת בַּרְזֶל	gelulot barzel
laxative	מְשַׁלְשֵׁל	meshalshel
mouthwash	נוֹזֵל לִשְׁטִיפַת הַפֶּה	nozel lishtifat hape
sanitary napkins	תַּחְבּוֹשׁוֹת הִיגְיֶנִיּוֹת	tahboshot higieniyot
sedative	תְּרוּפַת הַרְגָּעָה	terufat hargaa
sleeping pills	גְּלוּלוֹת שֵׁנָה	gelulot sheyna
stomach pills	גְּלוּלוֹת לִכְאֵב בֶּטֶן	gelulot likeev beten
thermometer	מַדְחוֹם	madhom
throat lozenges	טַבְלֵטִים נֶגֶד כְּאֵב גָּרוֹן	tabletim neged keev garon
tissues	מִטְפָּחוֹת נְיָר	mitpahot neyar
tonic	תְּרוּפַת עִדּוּד	terufat idud
tranquilizers	גְּלוּלַת הַרְגָּעָה	gelulat hargaa
vitamin pills	גְּלוּלַת וִיטָמִין	gelulat vitamin

Part 2—Toiletry

I'd like a/an/some . . .	. . . אֲנִי רוֹצֶה	ani rotze/ani rotza
acne cream	מִשְׁחָה נֶגֶד פִּצְעֵי בַּגְרוּת	mishḥa neged pitzey bagru
after-shave lotion	מֵי גִלוּחַ	mey giluaḥ
astringent	מֵי פָּנִים	mey panim
bath salts	מְלָחִים לְאַמְבַּטְיָה	melaḥim leambatya
cleansing tissue	מַפִּיוֹת נִגוּב	mapiyot niguv
cream	קְרֶם	krem
cleansing cream	לְנִקּוּי הַפָּנִים	lenikuy hapanim
cuticle cream	לְקְרוּם הַצִּפָּרְנַיִם	likrum hatzipornayim
enzyme cream	אֶנְזִימָטִי	enzimati
foundation cream	בָּסִיס לְאִפּוּר	basis leipur
moisturizing cream	לְרִכּוּךְ הָעוֹר	lerikukh haor
night cream	לַשֵּׁנָה	lasheyna
deodorant	דֵּאוֹדוֹרֶנְט	deodorant
eau de Cologne	מֵי קוֹלוֹן	mey kolon
eye pencil	מִכְחוֹל לִצְבִיעַת עֵינַיִם	mikhḥol litzviat eynayim
eye shadow	צֶבַע לְעַפְעַפַּיִם	tzeva leafapayim
face powder	פּוּדְרָה לַפָּנִים	pudra lapanim
foot cream	מִשְׁחָה לָרַגְלַיִם	mishḥa laraglayim
hand cream	לַיָּדַיִם	layadayim
lipsalve	מִשְׁחָה לַשְּׂפָתַיִם	mishḥa lasfatayim
lipstick	שְׂפָתוֹן	sifton
lipstick brush	מִבְרֶשֶׁת שְׂפָתוֹן	mivreshet sifton
make-up bag	תִּיק אִפּוּר	tik ipur
make-up remover pads	כָּרִיּוֹת לְהוֹרָדַת אִפּוּר	kariyot lehoradat ipur
nail brush	מִבְרֶשֶׁת לְצִפָּרְנַיִם	mivreshet letzipornayim
nail clippers	גּוֹזֵז צִפָּרְנַיִם	gozez tzipornayim
nail file	פְּצִירָה לְצִפָּרְנַיִם	petzira letzipornayim
nail-lacquer remover	תַּכְשִׁיר לְהוֹרָדַת לַכָּה	takhshir lehoradat laka
nail polish	לַכָּה לְצִפָּרְנַיִם	laka letzipornayim
nail scissors	מִסְפָּרַיִם לְצִפָּרְנַיִם	misparayim letzipornayim

nail strengthener	מְחַזֵק צִפָּרְנַיִם	mehazek tzipornayim
perfume	בּוֹשֶׂם	bosem
powder	פּוּדְרָה	pudra
powder box	פּוּדְרִיָּה	pudriya
razor blades	סַכִּינֵי גִלּוּחַ	sakiney giluah
rouge	אֹדֶם	odem
cream/powder	בְּמִשְׁחָה / בְּאַבְקָה	bemishha/beavka
shampoo	שַׁמְפּוּ	shampo
shaver	מְכוֹנַת גִלּוּחַ	mekhonat giluah
shaving brush	מִבְרֶשֶׁת גִלּוּחַ	mivreshet giluah
shaving cream	מִשְׁחַת גִלּוּחַ	mishhat giluah
shaving soap	סַבּוֹן גִלּוּחַ	sabon giluah
soap	סַבּוֹן	sabon
sun-tan cream	קְרֶם שִׁזּוּף	krem shizuf
sun-tan oil	שֶׁמֶן שִׁזּוּף	shemen shizuf
talcum powder	טַלְק	talk
toilet bag	תִּיק רַחְצָה	tik rahtza
toilet paper	נְיָר טוּאָלֶט	neyar tualet
toothbrush	מִבְרֶשֶׁת שִׁנַּיִם	mivreshet shinayim
toothpaste	מִשְׁחַת שִׁנַּיִם	mishhat shinayim
towel	מַגֶּבֶת	megevet
wash-off face cleanser	נוֹזֵל לַהֲסָרַת אִפּוּר	nozel lehasarat ipur

For your hair

brush	מִבְרֶשֶׁת	mivreshet
colouring	צֶבַע	tzeva
comb	מַסְרֵק	masrek
curlers	גַּלְגַּלִּים לַשֵּׂעָר	galgalim lesear
grips	מֶלְקָחַיִם לַשֵּׂעָר	melkahaim lesear
lacquer	לַכָּה	laka
piece	פֵּאָה נוֹכְרִית	pea nokhrit
pins	סִכּוֹת רֹאשׁ	sikot rosh

Clothing

If you want to buy something specific, prepare yourself in advance. Look at the list of clothing on page 117. Get some idea of the colour, material and size you want. They're all listed in the next few pages.

SHOPPING GUIDE

General

I'd like . . .	הָיִיתִי רוֹצֶה...	hayiti rotze
I want . . . for a 10-year-old boy.	אֲנִי רוֹצֶה...לְיֶלֶד בֶּן עֶשֶׂר.	ani rotze . . . leyeled ben eser
I want something like this.	אֲנִי רוֹצֶה מַשֶּׁהוּ כָּזֶה.	ani rotze mashehu kaze
I like the one in the window.	אֲנִי רוֹצֶה כָּזֶה שֶׁבַּחַלּוֹן.	ani rotze kaze shebahalon
How much is that per metre?	כַּמָּה עוֹלֶה הַמֶּטֶר?	kama ole hameter

1 centimetre =	0.39 in.	1 inch = 2.54 cm.
1 metre	= 39.37 in.	1 foot = 30.5 cm.
10 metres	= 32.81 ft.	1 yard = 0.91 m.

Colour

I want something in . . .	אֲנִי רוֹצֶה מַשֶּׁהוּ בְּ...	ani rotze mashehu be
I want a darker shade.	מַשֶּׁהוּ יוֹתֵר כֵּהֶה, בְּבַקָּשָׁה.	mashehu yoter kehe, bevakasha
I want something to match this.	מַשֶּׁהוּ שֶׁתְּאִים לָזֶה, בְּבַקָּשָׁה.	mashehu sheyatim laze, bevakasha
I don't like the colour.	הַצֶּבַע הַזֶּה לֹא מוֹצֵא חֵן בְּעֵינַי.	hatzeva haze lo motze hen beeynay

beige	בֶּז'	bezh
black	שָׁחוֹר	shahor
blue	כָּחוֹל	kahol
brown	חוּם	hum
cream	קְרֶם	krem
emerald	יָרוֹק בָּהִיר	yarok bahir
gold	זָהָב	zahav
green	יָרוֹק	yarok
grey	אָפוֹר	afor
mauve	אָדוֹם כֵּהֶה	adom kehe
orange	כָּתוֹם	katom
pink	וָרוֹד	varod
purple	אַרְגָּמָן	argaman
red	אָדוֹם	adom
scarlet	שָׁנִי	shani
silver	כֶּסֶף	kesef
white	לָבָן	lavan
yellow	צָהוֹב	tzahov

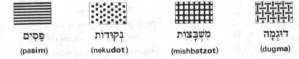

| פַּסִים | נְקוּדוֹת | מִשְׁבָּצוֹת | דֻגְמָה |
| (pasim) | (nekudot) | (mishbatzot) | (dugma) |

Material

Have you anything in . . . ?	יֵשׁ לְךָ מַשֶּׁהוּ בְּ...?	yesh lekha mashehu be
Is that made here?	הַאִם זֶה תּוֹצֶרֶת הָאָרֶץ?	haim ze totzeret haaretz
hand-made	עֲבוֹדַת יָד.	avodat yad
imported	יְבוּא	yevu
Have you any better quality?	יֵשׁ לְךָ מַשֶּׁהוּ טוֹב יוֹתֵר?	yesh lekha mashehu tov yoter

What's it made of?	מִמַּה זֶה עָשׂוּי?	mima ze asuy
cambric	בַּד כּוּתְנָה עָדִין	bad kutna adin
camel hair	שֵׂעַר גָּמָל	sear gamal
chiffon	שִׁפוֹן	shifon
corduroy	קוֹרְדְּרוֹי	korderoy
cotton	כּוּתְנָה	kutna
felt	לֶבֶד	leved
flannel	פְלָאנֶל	flanel
gabardine	גַּבַּרְדִין	gabardin
lace	תַחֲרִים	taharim
leather	עוֹר	or
linen	פִּשְׁתָּן	pishtan
pique	פִּיקֶה	pika
poplin	פּוֹפְלִין	poplin
rayon	זְהוֹרִית	zehorit
rubber	גּוּמִי	gumi
silk	מֶשִׁי	meshi
suede	זָמְשׁ	zamsh
taffeta	טַפְטָה	tafeta
towelling	בַּד מַגֶּבֶת	bad magevet
velvet	קְטִיפָה	ketifa
velveteen	חִקּוּי קְטִיפָה	hikuy ketifa
wool	בַּד צֶמֶר	bad **tzemer**
worsted	בַּד צֶמֶר סָרוּק	bad **tzemer** saruk

Size

My size is . . .	הַמִּידָה שֶׁלִּי. . .	hamida sheli
I don't know the Israeli sizes.	אֵינֶנִּי מַכִּיר אֶת הַמִּידוֹת בְּיִשְׂרָאֵל.	eyneni makir et hamidot belsrael

In that case, look at the charts on the next page.

This is your size

Ladies

Dresses/suits					
American	10	12	14	16	18	20
British	32	34	36	38	40	42
Israeli	38	40	42	44	46	48

	Stockings						Shoes			
American	8	8½	9	9½	10	10½	6	7	8	9
British							4½	5½	6½	7½
Israeli	0	1	2	3	4	5	37	38	38½	40

Gentlemen

	Suits/overcoats						Shirts			
American	36	38	40	42	44	46	15	16	17	18
British										
Israeli	46	48	50	52	54	56	39	41	43	45

	Shoes								
American	5	6	7	8	8½	9	9½	10	11
British									
Israeli	38	39	41	42	43	43	44	44	45

A good fit?

Can I try it on?	אוּכַל לִמְדוֹד אֶת זֶה?	ukhal limdod et ze
Where's the fitting room?	אֵיפֹה אוּכַל לִמְדוֹד אֶת זֶה?	eyfo ukhal limdod et ze
Is there a mirror?	יֵשׁ שָׁם רְאִי?	yesh sham rei
Does it fit?	זֶה מוּנָח טוֹב עָלַי?	ze munaḥ tov alay

FOR NUMBERS, see page 175

SHOPPING GUIDE

It fits very well.	זֶה מַתְאִים לִי בְּדִיּוּק.	ze matim li bediyuk
It doesn't fit.	זֶה לֹא מַתְאִים לִי.	ze lo matim li
It's too . . .	זֶה יוֹתֵר מִדַּי...	ze yoter miday
short/long/tight/ loose	קָצָר / אָרוֹךְ / הָדוּק / רוֹפֵף	katzar/arokh/haduk/ rofef
How long will it take to alter?	כַּמָּה זְמַן יִקַּח הַתִּקּוּן?	kama zeman ikah hatikun

Shoes

I'd like a pair of . . .	אֲנִי רוֹצֶה זוּג...	ani rotze zug . . .
shoes/sandals/boots	נַעֲלַיִם / סַנְדָּלִים / נַעֲלַיִם גְּבוֹהוֹת	naalaim/sandalim naalaim gevohot
These are too . . .	הֵם יוֹתֵר מִדַּי...	hem yoter miday
narrow/wide	צָרִים / רְחָבִים	tzarim/rehavim
large/small	גְּדוֹלִים / קְטַנִּים	gedolim/ketanim
Do you have a larger size?	יֵשׁ לָכֶם מִסְפָּר יוֹתֵר גָּדוֹל?	yesh lakhem mispar yoter gadol
I want a smaller size.	אֲנִי רוֹצֶה מִסְפָּר יוֹתֵר קָטָן.	ani rotze mispar yoter katan
Do you have the same in . . . ?	יֵשׁ לָכֶם אוֹתוֹ דָּבָר בְּ...?	yesh lakhem oto davar be
brown/beige	חוּם / בֵּז'	hum/bezh
black/white	שָׁחוֹר / לָבָן	shahor/lavan

Shoes worn out? Here's the key to getting them fixed again . . .

Can you repair these shoes?	תּוּכַל לְתַקֵּן נַעֲלַיִם אֵלֶּה?	tukhal letaken naalaim ele
Can you stitch this?	תּוּכַל לִתְפּוֹר אֶת זֶה?	tukhal litpor et ze
I want new soles and heels.	אֲנִי רוֹצֶה סוּלְיוֹת וַעֲקֵבִים חֲדָשִׁים.	ani rotze sulyot vaakevim hadashim
When will they be ready?	מָתַי זֶה יִהְיֶה מוּכָן?	matay ze ihye mukhan

Clothes and accessories

I'd like a/an/some . . .	אֲנִי רוֹצֶה לִקְנוֹת...	ani rotze liknot
anorak	מְעִיל רוּחַ	meil ruaḥ
bathing cap	כּוֹבַע יָם	kova yam
bathing suit	בֶּגֶד יָם	beged yam
bath robe	חָלוּק רַחְצָה	ḥaluk raḥtza
blazer	מְעִיל סְפּוֹרְטִיבִי	meil sportivi
blouse	חֻלְצָה	ḥultza
bow tie	עֲנִיבַת פַּרְפָּר	anivat parpar
bra	חֲזִיָּה	ḥaziya
braces (Br.)	כְּתֵפִיּוֹת	ketefiyot
briefs	תַּחְתּוֹנִים לְגֶבֶר	taḥtonim legever
cap	כִּפָּה	kipa
cape	שִׁכְמִיָּה	shikhmiya
coat	ז'אקֶט	zhaket
costume	חֲלִיפָה	ḥalifa
dinner jacket	סְמוֹקִינְג	smoking
dress	שִׂמְלָה	simla
dressing gown	חָלוּק	ḥaluk
evening dress (woman's)	שִׂמְלַת עֶרֶב	simlat erev
dungarees	סַרְבָּל	sarbal
frock-coat	פְרַק	frak
fur coat	מְעִיל פַּרְוָה	meil parva
girdle	חֲגוֹרָה	ḥagora
gloves	כְּפָפוֹת	kefafot
handkerchief	מִמְחָטָה	mimḥata
hat	כּוֹבַע	kova
housecoat	מְעִיל בַּיִת	meil bayit
jacket	מִקְטֹרֶן	miktoren
jersey	אֲפֻדָּה	afuda
jumper (Br.)	סְוֶדֶר	sweder
lingerie	לְבָנִים לְאִשָּׁה	levanim leisha

mackintosh	מְעִיל גֶּשֶׁם	meil geshem
nightdress	כֻּתּוֹנֶת לַיְלָה	kutonet layla
overcoat	מְעִיל עֶלְיוֹן	meil elyon
panty-girdle	מָחוֹךְ	mahokh
pyjamas	פִּיזָ'מָה	pizhama
raincoat	מְעִיל גֶּשֶׁם	meil geshem
rubber boots	מַגָּפֵי גוּמִי	magafey gumi
sandals	סַנְדָּלִים	sandalim
scarf	מִטְפַּחַת רֹאשׁ	mitpahat rosh
shirt	חֻלְצָה	hultza
shoes	נַעֲלַיִם	naalaim
shorts (Br.)	מִכְנָסַיִם קְצָרִים	mikhnasaim ketzarim
skirt	חֲצָאִית	hatzait
sneakers	נַעֲלֵי סְפּוֹרְט	naaley sport
socks/stockings	גַּרְבַּיִם	garbaim
suit (men's)	חֲלִיפָה	halifa
sweater	סְוֶדֶר	sveder
swimsuit	בֶּגֶד יָם	beged yam
tennis shoes	נַעֲלֵי טֶנִיס	naaley tenis
tie	עֲנִיבָה	aniva
top coat	מְעִיל עֶלְיוֹן	meil elyon
trousers	מִכְנָסַיִם	mikhnasaim
underpants (men)	תַּחְתּוֹנִים	tahtonim legever
waistcoat	גִ'ילֶט	zhilet

belt	חֲגוֹרָה	hagora
buckle	אַבְזָם	avzam
button	כַּפְתּוֹר	kaftor
collar	צַוָּארוֹן	tzavaron
lapel	דַשׁ	dash
pocket	כִּיס	kis
zipper	רוּכְסָן	rukhsan

Electrical appliances and accessories—Records

The voltage is 220 volts AC—50 cycles. An adaptor plug may be useful.

What's the voltage?	מַה הַמֶּתַח בָּרֶשֶׁת?	ma hametaḥ bareshet
I want a plug for this . . .	אֲנִי רוֹצֶה תֶּקַע בִּשְׁבִיל . . .	ani rotze teka bishvil
Have you a battery for this . . . ?	יֵשׁ לָכֶם בַּטֶּרְיָה בִּשְׁבִיל . . . הַזֶּה?	yesh lakhem bateria bishvil . . . haze
This is broken. Can you repair it?	זֶה שָׁבוּר; תּוּכַל לְתַקֵּן זֹאת?	ze shavur; tukhal letaken zot
When will it be ready?	מָתַי זֶה יִהְיֶה מוּכָן?	matay ze ihye mukhan
I'd like a/an/some . . .	אֲנִי רוֹצֶה לִקְנוֹת . . .	ani rotze liknot
adaptor	מַחְלִיף זֶרֶם	maḥlif zerem
amplifier	מַגְבִּיר קוֹל	magbir kol
battery	בַּטֶּרְיָה	bateria
cassette	קַסֶּטָה	kaseta
clock	שָׁעוֹן	shaon
wall clock	שְׁעוֹן קִיר	sheon kir
food mixer	מִיקְסֶר	mikser
hair dryer	מְיַבֵּשׁ שֵׂעָר	moyabesh sear
iron	מַגְהֵץ	maghetz
kettle	קוּמְקוּם	kumkum
percolator	פֶּרְקוֹלַטוֹר	perkolator
plug	תֶּקַע	teka
radio	רַדְיוֹ	radio
car radio	לַמְכוֹנִית	limkhonit
portable radio	טְרַנְזִיסְטוֹר	transistor
record	תַּקְלִיט	taklit
record player	פַּטֶפוֹן	patefon
portable	מִטַּלְטֵל	mitaltel
shaver	מְכוֹנַת גִּלּוּחַ	mekhonat giluaḥ
speakers	רַמְקוֹלִים	ramkolim

tape recorder	רְשַׁם־קוֹל	reshamkol
cassette	לְקַסֵטוֹת	lakasetot
portable	מִטַלְטֵל	mitaltel
television	טֶלֶוִיזְיָה	televizia
portable	מְטַלְטֶלֶת	mitaltelet
toaster	טוֹסְטֶר	toster
transformer	שַׁנַאי	shanay

Record bar

Have you any records by . . . ?	?... יֵשׁ לָכֶם תַקְלִיט שֶׁל	yesh lakhem taklit shel
Can I listen to this record?	אֶפְשָׁר לִשְׁמוֹעַ תַקְלִיט זֶה זֶה?	efshar lishmoa taklit ze

אָרִיךְ נֶגֶן	arikh negen	LP
שְׁלֹשִׁים וְשָׁלֹשׁ	sheloshim veshalosh	33 rpm
אַרְבָּעִים וְחָמֵשׁ	arbaim vehamesh	45 rpm
מוֹנוֹ / סְטֶרֵיאוֹ	mono/stereo	mono/stereo

classical music	מוּסִיקָה קְלַסִית	musika klasit
folk music	שִׁירֵי עַם	shirey am
instrumental music	מוּסִיקָה אִינְסְטְרוּמֶנְטַלִית	musika instrumentalit
jazz	גַ'ז	jazz
light music	מוּסִיקָה קַלָה	musika kala
orchestral music	מוּסִיקָה תִזְמוֹרְתִית	musika tizmortit
pop music	פּוֹפּ	pop

Here are the names of a few popular recording artists known throughout Israel:

Hagashash Hahiver	Yehoram Gaon
Ilan Veilanit	Yafa Yarkoni
Boaz Sharabi	Avi Toledano
Shoshana Damari	Hava Albertstein
Mati Caspi	Yosi Banay

Men's hairdressing (barber)

I don't speak much Hebrew.	אֲנִי לֹא מְדַבֵּר טוֹב עִבְרִית.	ani lo medaber tov ivrit
I'm in a terrible hurry.	אֲנִי מְאֹד מְמַהֵר.	ani meod memaher
I want a haircut, please.	תִּסְפֹּרֶת, בְּבַקָּשָׁה.	tisporet, bevakasha
I'd like a shave.	גִּלּוּחַ, בְּבַקָּשָׁה.	giluah, bevakasha
Don't cut it too short.	אֲבַקֵּשׁ לֹא קָצָר מִדַּי.	avakesh lo katzar miday
Scissors only, please.	רַק בְּמִסְפָּרַיִם, בְּבַקָּשָׁה.	rak bemisparaim, bevakasha
A razor cut, please.	בְּתַעַר, בְּבַקָּשָׁה.	betaar, bevakasha
Don't use the clippers.	אֲבַקֵּשׁ בְּלִי מְכוֹנָה.	avakesh beli mekhona
Just a trim, please.	רַק לְיַשֵּׁר, בְּבַקָּשָׁה.	rak leyasher, bevakasha
That's enough off.	אַל תּוֹרִיד יוֹתֵר.	al torid yoter
A little more off the . . .	עוֹד קְצָת, בְּבַקָּשָׁה.	od ketzat, bevakasha
back	מֵאָחוֹר	meahor
neck	בָּעֹרֶף	baoref
sides	בַּצְּדָדִים	batzadadim
top	לְמַעְלָה	lemaala
I don't want any cream.	בְּלִי קְרֶם, בְּבַקָּשָׁה.	beli krem, bovakasha
Would you please trim my . . . ?	תּוּכַל לְיַשֵּׁר, בְּבַקָּשָׁה, אֶת . . .	tukhal leyasher, bevakasha, et
beard	הַזָּקָן	hazakan
moustache	הַשָּׂפָם	hasafam
sideboards (sideburns)	הַפֵּאוֹת	hapeyot
Thank you. That's fine.	תּוֹדָה, זֶה בְּסֵדֶר גָּמוּר.	toda, ze beseyder gamur
How much do I owe you?	כַּמָּה אֲנִי חַיָּב לְךָ?	kama ani hayav lekha
This is for you.	זֶה בִּשְׁבִילְךָ.	ze bishvilkha

One pound would be a fair tip.

Ladies' hairdressing

Can I make an appointment for some time on Thursday?	אֲנִי רוֹצָה לְהַזְמִין תּוֹר לְיוֹם חֲמִישִׁי.	ani rotza lehazmin tor leyom ḥamishi
I'd like it cut and shaped.	אֲנִי רוֹצָה תִּסְפֹּרֶת וְתִסְרֹקֶת.	ani rotza tisporet vetisroket
with a fringe	עִם שׁוּלַיִים	im shulaim
page-boy style	תִּסְפֹּרֶת נַעַר	tisporet naar
a razor cut	בְּתַעַר	betaar
a re-style	תִּסְפֹּרֶת חֲדָשָׁה	tisporet ḥadasha
a permanent	סִלְסוּל	silsul
with ringlets	תַּלְתַּלִים	taltalim
with waves	גַּלִים	galim
in a bun	קוּקוּ	kuku
I want a . . .	אֲנִי רוֹצָה . . .	ani rotza
bleach	לְהוֹרִיד אֶת הַצֶּבַע	lehorid et hatzeva
colour rinse	שְׁטִיפָה	shetifa
dye	צְבִיעָה	zevia
shampoo and set	חֲפִיפָה וְסִדוּר שְׂעָרוֹת	ḥafifa vesidur searot
touch up	תִּקּוּן קַל	tikun kal
the same colour	אוֹתוֹ צֶבַע	oto tzeva
a darker colour	יוֹתֵר כֵּהֶה	yoter kehe
a lighter colour	יוֹתֵר בָּהִיר	yoter bahir
auburn/blond/ brunette	אֲדַמְדַם / בְּלוֹנְד / שָׁטֶן	adamdam/blond/ shaten
Do you have a colour chart?	יֵשׁ לָךְ דוּגְמָאוֹת צְבָעִים?	yesh lakh dugmaot tzevaim
I want a . . .	אֲנִי רוֹצָה . . .	ani rotza . . .
manicure/pedicure/ face-pack	מַנִיקוּר / פֶּדִיקוּר / טִפּוּל פָּנִים.	manikur/pedikur/ tipul panim

Tipping: one pound.

Jeweller's—Watchmaker's

Diamond cutting is one of the most important trades of Israel, and free tours to diamond-cutting factories are offered throughout the year. Arrangements for a visit can be made at hotels or at the tourist office.

Asking

Can you repair this watch?	תּוּכַל לְתַקֵּן אֶת הַשָּׁעוֹן הַזֶּה?	tukhal letaken et hashaon haze
The . . . is broken.	הַ. . . שָׁבוּר.	ha . . . shavur
glass/spring	זְכוּכִית / קְפִיץ	zezukhit/kefitz
I want this watch cleaned.	אֲנִי רוֹצֶה לִמְסוֹר אֶת הַשָּׁעוֹן לְנִקּוּי.	ani rotze limsor et hashaon lenikuy
When will it be ready?	מָתַי זֶה יִהְיֶה מוּכָן?	matay ze ihye mukhan
Could I see that, please?	אֶפְשָׁר לִרְאוֹת אֶת זֶה, בְּבַקָּשָׁה?	efshar lirot et ze, bevakasha
I'm just looking around.	אֲנִי רַק מִסְתַּכֵּל.	ani rak mistakel
I want a small present for . . .	אֲנִי רוֹצֶה מַתָּנָה קְטַנָּה בִּשְׁבִיל . . .	ani rotze matana ketana bishvil
I don't want anything too expensive.	לֹא יָקָר מִדַּי.	lo yakar miday
I want something . . .	אֲנִי רוֹצֶה מַשֶּׁהוּ . . .	ani rotze mashehu
better/cheaper/ simpler	טוֹב יוֹתֵר / זוֹל יוֹתֵר / פָּשׁוּט יוֹתֵר	tov yoter/zol yoter/ pashut yoter
Have you anything in gold?	יֵשׁ לְךָ מַשֶּׁהוּ בְּזָהָב?	yesh lekha mashehu bezahav
Is this real silver?	זֶה כֶּסֶף אֲמִיתִי?	ze kesef amiti

If it's made of gold, ask:

| How many carats is this? | כַּמָּה קָרָט? | kama karat |

When you go to a jeweller's, you've probably got some idea of what you want beforehand. Find out what the article is made of and then look up the Hebrew name for the article itself in the following lists.

What's it made of ?

amber	עַנְבָּר	inbar
amethyst	אַחְלָמָה	ahlama
chromium	כְּרוֹם	krom
copper	נְחֹשֶׁת	nehoshet
coral	אַלְמֹג	almog
crystal	גָּבִישׁ	gavish
cut-glass	זְכוּכִית מְלֻטֶּשֶׁת	zekhukhit meluteshet
diamond	יַהֲלוֹם	yahalom
emerald	בָּרֶקֶת	bareket
enamel	אֵימָל	emal
glass	זְכוּכִית	zekhukhit
gold	זָהָב	zahav
gold-leaf	עֲלֵה זָהָב	ale zahav
ivory	שֶׁנְהָב	shenhav
jade	יַרְקָן	yarkan
onyx	שֹׁהַם	shoham
pearl	פְּנִינָה	penina
pewter	בְּדִיל־עוֹפֶרֶת	bedil oferet
platinum	פְּלָטִינָה	platina
ruby	אֹדֶם	odem
sapphire	סַפִּיר	sapir
silver	כֶּסֶף	kesef
silver-plate	צִפּוּי כֶּסֶף	tzipuy kesef
stainless steel	פְּלָדָה לֹא מַחְלִידָה	pelada lo mahlida
topaz	טוֹפָז	topaz
turquoise	טוּרְקִיז	turkiz

What is it?

I'd like a/an/some . . .	אֲבַקֵשׁ . . .	avakesh
beads	חֲרוּזִים	haruzim
bracelet	צָמִיד	tzamid
charm bracelet	צָמִיד עִם קָמֵעַ	tzamid im kamea
brooch	סִכַּת נוֹי	sikat noy
chain	שַׁרְשֶׁרֶת	sharsheret
charm	קָמֵעַ	kamea
cigarette case	נַרְתִּיק לְסִגָרִיוֹת	nartik lesigariyot
cigarette lighter	מַצִּית	matzit
clock	שָׁעוֹן	shaon
alarm clock	שָׁעוֹן מְעוֹרֵר	shaon meorer
travel clock	שָׁעוֹן עִם מַעֲמָד	shaon im maamad
cross	צְלָב	tzelav
cuff-links	חֲפָתִים	hafatim
cutlery	סַכּוּ"ם	sakum
earrings	עֲגִילִים	agilim
necklace	מַחֲרוֹזֶת	maharozet
pendant	תַּלְיוֹן	talyon
pin	סִכָּה	sika
powder compact	פּוּדְרִיָּה	pudriya
ring	טַבַּעַת	tabaat
engagement ring	טַבַּעַת אֵירוּסִין	tabaat eyrusin
signet ring	טַבַּעַת חוֹתָם	tabaat hotam
wedding ring	טַבַּעַת נִשּׂוּאִין	tabaat nisuin
rosary	מַחֲרוֹזֶת תְּפִילָה	maharozet tefila
silverware	כְּלֵי כֶּסֶף	keley kesef
strap	רְצוּעָה	retzua
watch strap	רְצוּעַת שָׁעוֹן	retzuat shaon
tie-clip/tie-pin	סִכָּה לְעֲנִיבָה	sika laaniva
watch	שָׁעוֹן	shaon
pocket watch	שְׁעוֹן כִּיס	sheon kis
wrist-watch	שְׁעוֹן יָד	sheon yad

SHOPPING GUIDE

Laundry—Dry cleaning

If your hotel doesn't have its own laundry/dry cleaning service, ask the porter:

Where's the nearest laundry?	אֵיפֹה הַמַּכְבֵּסָה הַקְּרוֹבָה בְּיוֹתֵר?	eyfo hamakhbesa hakerova beyoter
I want these clothes . . .	אֲנִי רוֹצֶה לִמְסֹר בְּגָדִים אֵלֶה לְ ...	ani rotze limsor begadim ele le
cleaned	נִקּוּי	nikuy
pressed/ironed	גִּהוּץ	gihutz
washed	כְּבִיסָה	kevisa
When will it be ready?	מָתַי זֶה יִהְיֶה מוּכָן?	matay ze ihye mukhan
I need it . . .	אֲנִי צָרִיךְ אֶת זֶה...	ani tzarikh et ze
today	הַיּוֹם	hayom
tonight	הַלַּיְלָה	halayla
tomorrow	מָחָר	mahar
before Friday	לִפְנֵי יוֹם שִׁשִּׁי	lifney yom shishi
I want it as soon as possible.	אֲנִי רוֹצֶה אֶת זֶה בְּהֶקְדֵּם הָאֶפְשָׁרִי.	ani rotze et ze bahekdem haefshari
Can you . . . this?	תּוּכַל... אֶת זֶה?	tukhal . . . et ze
mend/stitch	לְתַקֵּן/לִתְפֹּר	letaken/litpor
Can you sew on this button?	תּוּכַל לִתְפֹּר אֶת הַכַּפְתּוֹר הַזֶּה?	tukhal litpor et hakaftor haze
Can you get this stain out?	תּוּכַל לְהוֹרִיד אֶת הַכֶּתֶם הַזֶּה?	tukhal lehorid et haketem haze
Can this be invisibly mended?	אֶפְשָׁר לְתַקֵּן אֶת זֶה שֶׁלֹּא יוּרְגַּשׁ?	efshar letaken et ze shelo yurgash
This isn't mine.	זֶה לֹא שֶׁלִּי.	ze lo sheli
Where's my laundry?	אֵיפֹה הַכְּבִיסָה שֶׁלִּי?	eyfo hakevisa sheli
You promised it for today.	הִבְטַחְתָּ אוֹתָהּ לְהַיּוֹם.	livtahta ota lehayom

Photography—Cameras

The basic still and home movie exposures are given in English in the instructions with the roll.

I want an inexpensive camera.	אֲנִי רוֹצֶה מַצְלֵמָה זוֹלָה.	ani rotze matzlema zola

Film

I'd like a . . .	אֲבַקֵּשׁ . . .	avakesh
film for this camera	סֶרֶט לְמַצְלֵמָה זֹאת	seret lematzlema zot
120 film	סֶרֶט מֵאָה וְעֶשְׂרִים	seret mea veesrim
127 film	סֶרֶט מֵאָה עֶשְׂרִים וְשֶׁבַע	seret mea esrim vesheva
135 film	סֶרֶט מֵאָה שְׁלוֹשִׁים וְחָמֵשׁ	seret mea sheloshim vehamesh
8-mm film	סֶרֶט שֶׁל שְׁמוֹנָה מִילִימֶטֶר	seret shel shemona milimeter
super 8	סוּפֶּר שְׁמוֹנָה	super shemona
35-mm film	סֶרֶט שֶׁל שְׁלוֹשִׁים וְחֲמִשָּׁה מִילִימֶטֶר	seret shel sheloshim vehamisha milimeter
620 (6 x 6) roll film	סֶרֶט שֵׁשׁ מֵאוֹת וְעֶשְׂרִים	seret shesh meot veesrim
20/36 exposures	עֶשְׂרִים / שְׁלוֹשִׁים וָשֵׁשׁ תְּמוּנוֹת	esrim/sheloshim veshesh temunot
this size	בְּגֹדֶל זֶה	begodel ze
this ASA/DIN number	אַסָא / דִין זֶה	ASA/DIN ze
black and white	שָׁחוֹר לָבָן	shahor lavan
colour	צִבְעוֹנִי	tzivoni
colour negative	נֶגָטִיב צִבְעוֹנִי	negativ tzivoni
colour reversal	הִפּוּךְ צְבָעִים	hipukh tzevaim
colour slide (transparency)	שְׁקוּפִית צִבְעוֹנִית	shekufit tzivonit
artificial light type (indoor)	לְאוֹר מְלָאכוּתִי	leor melakhuti
daylight type (outdoor)	לְאוֹר הַשֶּׁמֶשׁ	leor hashemesh
Does this price include processing?	הַאִם הַמְחִיר כּוֹלֵל פִּתּוּחַ?	haim hamehir kolel pituah

FOR NUMBERS, see page 175

SHOPPING GUIDE

Processing

How much do you charge for developing?	כַּמָּה עוֹלֶה פִּתּוּחַ?	kama ole pituaḥ
I want . . . prints of each negative.	אֲנִי רוֹצֶה . . . תְּמוּנוֹת מִכָּל נֶגָטִיב.	ani rotze . . . temunot mikol negativ

Accessories

I want a/an/some . . .	אֲבַקֵּשׁ . . .	avakesh
cable release	חוּט הַפְעָלָה	ḥut hafala
exposure meter	מַד חֲשִׂיפָה	mad ḥasifa
flash bulbs	נוּרוֹת הַבְזָקָה	nurot havzaka
for black and white	לְשָׁחוֹר לָבָן	leshaḥor lavan
for colour	לִצְבָעִים	litzvaim
filter	פִילְטֶר	filter
red/yellow	אָדֹם / צָהֹב	adom/tzahov
ultra violet	אוּלְטְרָה סָגוֹל	ultra segol
lens	עֲדָשָׁה	adasha
lens cap	כִּסּוּי לָעֲדָשָׁה	kisuy laadasha
lens cleaners	מַטְלִית לָעֲדָשָׁה	matlit laadasha
tripod	תְּלַת־רֶגֶל	telat regel

Broken

This camera doesn't work. Can you repair it?	הַמַּצְלֵמָה מְקוּלְקֶלֶת, תּוּכַל לְתַקֵּן אוֹתָה?	hamatzlema mekulkelet, tukhal letaken ota
The film is jammed.	הַסֶּרֶט נִתְפַּס.	haseret nitpas
There's something wrong with the . . .	מַשֶּׁהוּ לֹא בְּסֵדֶר עִם . . .	mashehu lo beseyder im
exposure counter	הַמַּד חֲשִׂיפָה	hamad ḥasifa
film winder	הַסְּלִיל	haslil
light meter	הַמַּד אוֹר	hamad or
shutter	הַסֶּגֶר	haseger

Provisions

Here is a list of basic food and drink that you might want on a picnic or for the occasional meal at home.

I'd like a/an/some . . ., please.	. . . אֲנִי רוֹצֶה לִקְנוֹת	ani rotze liknot
apples	תַּפּוּחִים	tapuhim
bananas	בַּנָנוֹת	bananot
biscuits	בִּסְקְוִיטִים	biskvitim
bread	לֶחֶם	lehem
butter	חֶמְאָה	hema
cake	עוּגָה	uga
cheese	גְבִינָה	gevina
chocolate	שׁוֹקוֹלָד	shokolad
coffee	קָפֶה	kafe
cold meat	בָּשָׂר קָפוּא	basar kafu
cookies	עוּגִיּוֹת	ugiyot
cooking fat	שׁוּמָן בִּשּׁוּל	shuman bishul
crisps	פְּרִיכִים	perikhim
cucumbers	מְלָפְפוֹנִים	melafefonim
frankfurters	נַקְנִיקִיּוֹת	naknikiyot
ice-cream	גְלִידָה	gelida
lemonade	לִימוֹנָדָה	limonada
lemons	לִימוֹנִים	limonim
lettuce	חַסָּה	hasa
liver sausage	נַקְנִיק כָּבֵד	naknik kaved
milk	חָלָב	halav
mustard	חַרְדָּל	hardal
oranges	תַּפּוּזִים	tapuzim
pâté	מִמְרָח	mimrah
pepper	פִּלְפֵּל	pilpel
pickles	חֲמוּצִים	hamutzim
potatoes	תַּפּוּחֵי אֲדָמָה	tapuhey adama
rolls	לַחְמָנִיּוֹת	lahmaniyot

salad	סָלָט	salat
sausages	נַקְנִיק	naknik
sugar	סוּכָּר	sukar
sweets	סוּכָּרִיוֹת	sukariyot
tea	תֵה	tey
tomatoes	עַגְבָנִיוֹת	agvaniyot

And don't forget . . .

a bottle opener	פּוֹתְחָן בַּקְבּוּקִים	pothan bakbukim
a corkscrew	מַחְלֵץ לִפְקָקִים	mahletz lipkakim
matches	גַפְרוּרִים	gafrurim
paper napkins	מַפִּיוֹת	mapiyot
a can opener	פּוֹתְחָן קוּפְסָאוֹת	pothan kufsaot

Weights and measures

1 kilogram or kilo (kg) = 1000 grams (g)	
100 g = 3.5 oz.	½ kg = 1.1 lb.
200 g = 7.0 oz.	1 kg = 2.2 lb.
1 oz. = 28.35 g	
1 lb. = 453.60 g	

1 litre (l) = 0.88 imp. quarts = 1.06 U.S. quarts
1 imp. quart = 1.14 l   1 U.S. quart = 0.95 l
1 imp. gallon = 4.55 l   1 U.S. gallon = 3.8 l

---

barrel	חָבִית	havit
box	קוּפְסָה	kufsa
can	קוּפְסָה	kufsa
carton	קַרְטוֹן	karton
crate	אַרְגָּז	argaz
jar	צִנְצֶנֶת	tzintzenet
packet	חֲבִילָה	havila
tin	קוּפְסָה	kufsa
tube	שְׁפוֹפֶרֶת	shefoferet

Souvenirs

Israel is one of the rare countries which have modern up-to-date shopping centres and supermarkets with fixed prices right beside old bazaars where haggling is a must. You'll find everything in Israel, starting with electrical appliances and ending with ancient statues and pictures. Depending on your luck and skill, you may find unexpected bargains. Here's a short list of items to look for in Israel.

antiques	עַתִּיקוֹת	atikot
backgammon	שֵׁשׁ־בֵּשׁ	shesh-besh
baskets	סַלִים	salim
books	סְפָרִים	sefarim
carpets	שְׁטִיחִים	shetihim
copper and brass	כְּלֵי נְחוֹשֶׁת	keley nehoshet
ceramics	קֶרָמִיקָה	keramika
diamonds	יַהֲלוֹמִים	yahalomim
furs	פַּרְווֹת	parvot
glass	זְכוּכִית	zekhukhit
handicrafts	עֲבוֹדוֹת יָד	avodot yad
jewellery	תַּכְשִׁיטִים	takhshitim
nargilah (oriental pipe)	נַרְגִּילָה	nargila
olivewood	עֲבוֹדוֹת מֵעֵץ זַיִת	avodot meetz zait
paintings	תְּמוּנוֹת	temunot
perfume	בּוֹשֶׂם	bosem
religious articles	תַּשְׁמִישֵׁי קְדֻשָּׁה	tashmishey kedusha
sandals	סַנְדָּלִים	sandalim
wines and liquors	יֵינוֹת וְלִיקֵרִים	yeynot velikerim

SOUVENIRS

... and oriental articles for which the Old City of Jerusalem with its narrow streets and small bazaars is highly recommended.

Tobacconist's

As at home, cigarettes are generally referred to by their brand names, e.g. Ascot. Brands that are manufactured locally are quite cheap. Foreign cigarettes are taxed and therefore more expensive.

TOBACCONIST'S

Buying

Give me a/an/ some . . ., please.	תֵּן לִי, בְּבַקָשָׁה...	ten li, bevakasha
cigars	סִיגָרִים	sigarim
cigarette case	נַרְתִּיק לְסִיגָרִיוֹת	nartik lesigariyot
cigarette holder	פִּיָה	piya
flints	אַבְנֵי מַצִית	avney matzit
lighter	מַצִית	matzit
lighter fluid/gas	בֶּנְזִין / גָז לְמַצִית	benzin/gaz lematzit
refill for a lighter	מִלּוּי	miluy
matches	גַפְרוּרִים	gafrurim
packet of cigarettes	קוּפְסַת סִיגָרִיוֹת	kufsat sigariyot
packet of Ascot	קוּפְסַת אֶסְקוֹט	kufsat Ascot
pipe	מִקְטֶרֶת	mikteret
pipe tobacco	טַבַּק לְמִקְטֶרֶת	tabak lemikteret
pipe cleaners	כְּלֵי נִקּוּי לְמִקְטֶרֶת	keley nikuy lemikteret
tobacco pouch	כִּיס טַבַּק	kis tabak
wick	פְּתִיל	petil
Have you any . . . ?	יֵשׁ לְךָ...?	yesh lekha
American cigarettes	סִיגָרִיוֹת אַמֶרִיקָאִיוֹת	sigariyot amerikaiyot
English cigarettes	סִיגָרִיוֹת אַנְגְלִיוֹת	sigariyot angliyot
menthol cigarettes	סִיגָרִיוֹת מֶנְתוֹל	sigariyot mentol
I'd like a carton.	תֵּן לִי קַרְטוֹן, בְּבַקָשָׁה	ten li karton, bevakasha

| filter-tipped | עִם פִּילְטֶר | im filter |
| without filter | בְּלִי פִּילְטֶר | beli filter |

While on the subject of cigarettes, suppose you want to offer somebody one?

Would you like a cigarette?	אַתָּה מְעַשֵּׁן?	ata meashen
Have one of mine.	קַח אַחַת מִשֶּׁלִּי.	kah ahat misheli
Try one of these. They're very mild.	נַסֵּה זֹאת; הִיא חַלָשָׁה מְאֹד.	nase zot; hi halasha meod
They're a bit strong.	הֵן קְצָת חֲזָקוֹת.	hen ketzat hazakot

And if somebody offers you one?

Thank you.	תּוֹדָה.	toda
No, thanks.	לֹא, תּוֹדָה.	lo, toda
I don't smoke.	אֲנִי לֹא מְעַשֵּׁן.	ani lo meashen
I've given it up.	הִפְסַקְתִּי לְעַשֵּׁן.	hifsakti leashen

Your money: banks—currency

At larger banks there's sure to be someone who speaks English. In most tourist centres you'll find small currency exchanges (banks), especially during high season. The exchange rates are the same everywhere. Remember to take your passport with you, as you may need it.

Hours

Business hours vary according to the season, but banks are normally open Sunday to Thursday from 8.30 a.m. to 12.30 p.m. and from 4 p.m. to 5.30 p.m; on Friday and days before Jewish holy days from 8.30 a.m. to noon.

Monetary unit

The Israeli monetary system is based on the *lira* (pound), divided into one hundred *agorot*. The normal abbreviation for Israeli currency is IL (ל״י) which means Israeli Lira.

There are coins of 1, 5, 10 and 25 agorot and of half a pound and 1 pound. Banknotes are for 1, 5, 10, 50 and 100 pounds. The one-pound banknote is gradually being replaced by the coin.

Before going

Where's the nearest bank?	אֵיפֹה הַבַּנק הַקָּרוֹב בְּיוֹתֵר?	eyfo habank hakarov beyoter
Where can I cash a traveller's cheque (check)?	אֵיפֹה אֶפְשָׁר לִפְדּוֹת הַמְחָאוֹת נוֹסְעִים?	eyfo efshar lifdot hamḥaot nosim
Where's the American Express?	אֵיפֹה הַ״אמריקן אקספרס״?	eyfo haAmerican Express

Inside

I want to change some dollars.	אֲנִי רוֹצֶה לְהַחְלִיף כַּמָה דוֹלָרִים.	ani rotze lehaḥlif kama dolarim
I'd like to change some pounds.	אֲנִי רוֹצֶה לְהַחְלִיף כַּמָה לִירוֹת סְטֶרְלִינְג.	ani rotze lehaḥlif kama lirot sterling
Here's my passport.	הִנֵּה הַדַּרְכּוֹן שֶׁלִּי.	hine hadarkon sheli
What's the exchange rate?	מַהוּ שַׁעַר הַחֲלִיפִין?	mahu shaar haḥalifin
What rate of commission do you charge?	מַהוּ הַקּוֹמִיסְיוֹן שֶׁאַתֶּם לוֹקְחִים?	mahu hakomisyon sheatem lokhim
Can you cash a personal cheque?	אַתֶּם מְקַבְּלִים צֶ׳קִים פְּרָטִים?	atem mekabelim chekim pratiim
How long will it take to clear?	כַּמָה זְמַן יִקַּח לִבְדּוֹק?	kama zeman ikah livdok
Can you cable my bank in London?	תּוּכַל לִשְׁלוֹחַ מִבְרָק לַבַּנְק שֶׁלִּי בְּלוֹנְדוֹן?	tukhal lishloaḥ mivrak labank sheli beLondon
I have a letter of credit.	יֵשׁ לִי מִכְתָּב אַשְׁרַאי.	yesh li mikhtav ashray
an introduction from . . .	מִכְתָּב הַמְלָצָה מִ . . .	mikhtav hamlatza mi
a credit card	כַּרְטִיס אַשְׁרַאי	kartis ashray
I'm expecting some money from England. Has it arrived yet?	אֲנִי מְחַכֶּה לְכֶסֶף מֵאַנְגְּלִיָּה; כְּבָר הִגִּיעַ?	ani meḥake lekesef kevar higia meAnglia
Give me four 100 pound notes (bills) and some small change, please.	תֵּן לִי אַרְבָּעָה שְׁטָרוֹת שֶׁל מֵאָה לִירוֹת וּקְצָת כֶּסֶף קָטָן, בְּבַקָּשָׁה.	ten li arbaa shetarot shel mea lirot uktzat kesef katan, bevakasha
Give me six large notes and the rest in small notes.	תֵּן לִי שִׁשָּׁה שְׁטָרוֹת גְּדוֹלִים וְהַשְּׁאָר בִּשְׁטָרוֹת קְטַנִים.	ten li shisha shetarot gedolim vehashear bishtarot ketanim
Could you check that again, please?	תּוּכַל לִבְדּוֹק זֹאת שׁוּב, בְּבַקָּשָׁה.	tukhal livdok zot shuv bevakasha

BANKS

Depositing

I want to credit this to my account.	אֲנִי רוֹצֶה לְהַכְנִיס אֶת זֶה לַחֶשְׁבּוֹן שֶׁלִי.	ani rotze lehakhnis et ze laheshbon sheli
I want to credit this to Mr. Katz's account.	אֲנִי רוֹצֶה לְהַכְנִיס אֶת זֶה לַחֶשְׁבּוֹן שֶׁל מַר כַּץ.	ani rotze lehakhnis et ze laheshbon shel mar Katz
Where should I sign?	אֵיפֹה אֲנִי חוֹתֵם?	eyfo ani hotem

Currency converter

In a world of fluctuating currencies, we can offer no more than this do-it-yourself chart. You can get a card showing current exchange rates from banks, travel agents and tourist offices. Why not fill in this chart, too, for handy reference?

IL	£	$
50 agorot		
1 pound		
2 pounds		
3 pounds		
10 pounds		
25 pounds		
50 pounds		
75 pounds		
100 pounds		

FOR NUMBERS, see page 175

At the post office

In Israel, the post office is indicated by a white deer on a blue background. Mailboxes are red. The opening hours are from 8 a.m. to 6 p.m. (Sunday to Thursday) and from 8 a.m. to 2 p.m. on Fridays and days before Jewish holy days.

Where's the nearest post office?	אֵיפֹה מִשְׂרַד הַדֹּאַר הַקָּרוֹב בְּיוֹתֵר?	eyfo misrad hadoar hakarov beyoter
What time does the post office open?	מָתַי פּוֹתְחִים אֶת מִשְׂרַד הַדֹּאַר?	matay potehim et misrad hadoar
When does the post office close?	מָתַי סוֹגְרִים אֶת מִשְׂרַד הַדֹּאַר?	matay sogerim et misrad hadoar
What window do I go to for stamps?	בְּאֵיזֶה אֶשְׁנָב קוֹנִים בּוּלִים ?	beeyze eshnav konim bulim
At which counter can I cash an international money order?	בְּאֵיזֶה אֶשְׁנָב אֶפְשָׁר לִפְדוֹת הַמְחָאַת דֹּאַר בֵּינְלְאוּמִית?	beeyze eshnav efshar lifdot hamaḥaat doar beynleumit
I want some stamps please.	אֲבַקֵשׁ כַּמָּה בּוּלִים.	avakesh kama bulim
I want six 30 agorot stamps and four half-pound stamps.	אֲנִי רוֹצֶה שִׁשָּׁה בּוּלִים שֶׁל שְׁלוֹשִׁים אֲגוֹרוֹת וְאַרְבָּעָה שֶׁל חֲמִשִׁים אֲגוֹרוֹת.	ani rotze shisha bulim shel sheloshim agorot vearbaa shel ḥamishim agorot
What's the postage for a letter to England ?	כַּמָּה עוֹלֶה מִשְׁלוֹחַ מִכְתָּב לְאַנְגְלְיָה?	kama ole mishloaḥ mikhtav leAnglia
What's the postage for a postcard to the U.S.A. ?	כַּמָּה עוֹלֶה מִשְׁלוֹחַ גְלוּיָה לְאַרְצוֹת הַבְּרִית?	kama ole mishloaḥ geluya leArtzot Habrit
Do all letters go airmail?	הַאִם כָּל הַמִכְתָּבִים נִשְׁלָחִים בְּדֹּאַר אֲוִיר?	haim kol hamikhtavim nishlaḥim bedoar avir
I want to send this parcel.	אֲנִי רוֹצֶה לִשְׁלוֹחַ אֶת הַחֲבִילָה הַזֹּאת.	ani rotze lishloaḥ et haḥavila hazot

POST OFFICE

Do I need to fill in a customs declaration?	אֲנִי צָרִיךְ לְמַלֵּא הַצְהָרַת מֶכֶס?	ani tzarikh lemale hatzharat mekhes
I want to register this letter.	אֲנִי רוֹצֶה לִשְׁלֹחַ אֶת הַמִּכְתָּב הַזֶּה בְּדֹאַר רָשׁוּם.	ani rotze lishloaḥ et hamikhtav haze bedoar rashum
Where's the letter-box?	אֵיפֹה תֵּיבַת הַדֹּאַר?	eyfo teyvat hadoar
I want to send this by . . .	אֲנִי רוֹצֶה לִשְׁלֹחַ אֶת זֶה...	ani rotze lishloaḥ et ze
airmail	בְּדֹאַר אֲוִיר	bedoar avir
express (special delivery)	בְּדֹאַר אֶקְסְפְּרֶס	bedoar express
registered mail	בְּדֹאַר רָשׁוּם	bedoar rashum
Where is the poste restante (general delivery)?	אֵיפֹה הַדֹּאַר הַשָּׁמוּר?	eyfo hadoar hashamur
Is there any mail for me? My name is . . .	יֵשׁ דֹּאַר בִּשְׁבִילִי? שְׁמִי...	yesh doar bishvili? shemi
Here's my passport.	הִנֵּה הַדַּרְכּוֹן שֶׁלִּי.	hine hadarkon sheli

בּוּלִים	STAMPS
חֲבִילוֹת	PARCELS
הַמְחָאוֹת דֹּאַר	MONEY ORDERS

Cables (telegrams)

I want to send a cable (telegram). May I have a form, please?	אֲנִי רוֹצֶה לִשְׁלֹחַ מִבְרָק; אֶפְשָׁר לְקַבֵּל טֹפֶס, בְּבַקָּשָׁה?	ani rotze lishloaḥ mivrak; efshar lekabel tofes, bevakasha
How much is it per word?	כַּמָּה עוֹלָה מִלָּה?	kama ola mila
How long will a cable to Boston take?	תּוֹךְ כַּמָּה זְמַן מַגִּיעַ מִבְרָק לְבּוֹסְטוֹן?	tokh kama zeman magia mivrak leBoston

Telephoning

Most public telephones operate with tokens (*asimon*) which are for sale at post offices, kiosks etc. There are also public telephones in bars and cafés where a token isn't needed. These are indicated by the Israeli Postal Service emblem (a white deer on a blue background). For international communications call the telephone operator.

General

Where's the telephone?	אֵיפֹה הַטֶּלֶפוֹן?	eyfo hatelefon
Where's the nearest telephone booth?	אֵיפֹה הַטֶּלֶפוֹן הַצִבּוּרִי הַקָרוֹב בְּיוֹתֵר?	eyfo hatelefon hatziburi hakarov beyoter
May I use your phone?	אֶפְשָׁר לְהִשְׁתַּמֵשׁ בַּטֶלֶפוֹן?	efshar lehishtamesh betelefon
Have you a telephone directory in English?	יֵשׁ כָּאן מַדְרִיךְ טֶלֶפוֹן בְּאַנְגְלִית?	yesh kan madrikh telefon beanglit
Can you help me get this number?	תּוּכַל לַעֲזוֹר לִי לְהַשִׂיג מִסְפָּר זֶה?	tukhal laazor li lehasig mispar ze

Operator

Do you speak English?	אַת מְדַבֶּרֶת אַנְגְלִית?	at medaberet anglit
Good morning. I want Haifa 123456.	בֹּקֶר טוֹב, אֶפְשָׁר לְקַבֵּל חֵיפָה 123456.	boker tov, efshar lekabel Haifa 123456
Can I dial direct?	אֶפְשָׁר לְקַבֵּל שִׂיחָה יְשִׁירָה?	efshar lekabel siha yeshira
I want to reverse the charges.	אֲנִי רוֹצֶה שֶׁמְקַבֵּל הַשִׂיחָה יְשַׁלֵם.	ani rotze shemekabel hasiha yeshalem
Will you tell me the cost of the call afterwards?	תַּגִידִי לִי אַחַר כָּךְ מַה מְחִיר הַשִׂיחָה.	tagidi li ahar kakh ma mehir hasiha

TELEPHONE

Speaking

I want to speak to . . .	אֲנִי רוֹצֶה לְדַבֵּר עִם . . .	ani rotze ledaber im
Would you put me through to . . . ?	תּוּכְלִי לְהַעֲבִיר אוֹתִי אֶל . . .	tukhli lehaavir oti el
I want extension . . .	אֲבַקֵשׁ שְׁלוּחָה . . .	avakesh sheluha
Is that . . . ?	הַאִם זֶה . . . ?	haim ze
Hello. This is . . .	הָלוֹ, מְדַבֵּר . . .	halo, medaber

Bad luck

Would you try again later, please?	אַחַר כָּךְ תְּנַסִי שׁוּב, בְּבַקָשָׁה.	ahar kakh tenasi shuv, bevakasha
Operator, you gave me the wrong number.	סְלִיחָה, נָתַת לִי מִסְפָּר לֹא נָכוֹן.	seliha, natat li mispar lo nakhon

Not there

When will she be back?	מָתַי הִיא חוֹזֶרֶת?	matay hi hozeret
Will you tell her I called?	תּוּכְלִי לוֹמַר לָהּ שֶׁצִלְצַלְתִי?	tukhli lomar la shetziltzalti
My name's . . .	שְׁמִי . . .	shemi
Would you ask her to call me?	תּוּכְלִי לְבַקֵשׁ מִמֶנָה שֶׁתִתְקַשֵׁר אֵלַי?	tukhli levakesh mimena shetitkasher elay
Would you take a message, please?	אֶפְשָׁר לִמְסוֹר הוֹדָעָה, בְּבַקָשָׁה?	efshar limsor hodaa, bevakasha

Charges

What was the cost of that call?	כַּמָה עָלְתָה הַשִׂיחָה הַזֹאת?	kama alta hasiha hazot
I want to pay for the call.	אֲנִי רוֹצֶה לְשַׁלֵם בִּשְׁבִיל הַשִׂיחָה.	ani rotze leshalem bishvil hasiha

TELEPHONE

Possible answers

יֵשׁ לְךָ שִׂיחָה.	There's a telephone call for you.
רוֹצִים אוֹתְךָ בַּטֶּלֶפוֹן.	You're wanted on the telephone.
תַּמְתִּין עַל הַקַּו, בְּבַקָּשָׁה.	Hold the line, please.
תּוּכַל לְהַגְבִּיהַ אֶת הַקּוֹל, בְּבַקָּשָׁה?	Could you speak a bit louder, please?
מִי מְדַבֵּר?	Who's that speaking?
לְאֵיזֶה מִסְפָּר חִיַּגְתָּ?	What number are you calling?
הַקַּו תָּפוּס.	The line's engaged.
אֵין תְּשׁוּבָה.	There's no answer.
טָעוּת בְּמִסְפָּר.	You've got the wrong number.
הַטֶּלֶפוֹן לֹא פּוֹעֵל.	The phone is out of order.
הוּא יָצָא.	He's out at the moment.

TELEPHONE

The car

We'll start this section by considering your possible needs at a filling station.

Where's the nearest filling station?	אֵיפֹה תַחֲנַת הַדֶּלֶק הַקְּרוֹבָה בְּיוֹתֵר?	eyfo tahanat hadelek hakerova beyoter
I want . . . litres, please.	אֲנִי רוֹצֶה . . . לִיטֶר, בְּבַקָּשָׁה.	ani rotze . . . liter, bevakasha
ten/twenty/fifty	עֲשָׂרָה/עֶשְׂרִים/חֲמִשִּׁים	asara/esrim/hamishim
I want fifteen litres of standard/premium.	אֲנִי רוֹצֶה חֲמִשָּׁה עָשָׂר לִיטֶר רָגִיל / סוּפֶּר.	ani rotze hamisha asar liter ragil/super
Give me 10 pounds worth of . . .	תֵּן לִי דֶּלֶק בְּעֶשֶׂר לִירוֹת . . .	ten li delek beeser lirot
Fill her up, please.	מַלֵּא, בְּבַקָּשָׁה.	male, bevakasha
Check the oil and water, please.	תִּבְדֹּק שֶׁמֶן וּמַיִם, בְּבַקָּשָׁה.	tivdok shemen umayim, bevakasha
Give me . . . litres of oil.	תֵּן לִי . . . לִיטֶר שֶׁמֶן.	ten li . . . liter shemen
Top up (fill up) the battery with distilled water.	אֲבַקֵּשׁ מַיִם מְזֻקָּקִים לַמַּצְבֵּר.	avakesh mayim mezukakim lamatzber
Check the brake fluid.	תִּבְדּוֹק־נָא שֶׁמֶן בְּלָמִים (שֶׁמֶן בְּרֵייקָס).	tivdok na shemen balamim (shemen brakes)

Fluid measures					
litres	imp. gal.	U.S. gal.	litres	imp. gal.	U.S. gal.
5	1.1	1.3	30	6.6	7.8
10	2.2	2.6	35	7.7	9.1
15	3.3	3.9	40	8.8	10.4
20	4.4	5.2	45	9.9	11.7
25	5.5	6.5	50	11.0	13.0

Tire pressure			
lb./sq. in.	kg./cm.	lb./sq. in.	kg./cm.
10	0.7	26	1.8
12	0.8	27	1.9
15	1.1	28	2.0
18	1.3	30	2.1
20	1.4	33	2.3
21	1.5	36	2.5
23	1.6	38	2.7
24	1.7	40	2.8

Would you check the tires?	אַתָּה רוֹצֶה לִבְדוֹק אֶת הַגַּלְגַּלִּים?	ata rotze livdok et hagalgalim
The pressure should be one point six front, one point eight rear.	לַחַץ הָאֲוִיר צָרִיךְ לִהְיוֹת עֶשְׂרִים וְשָׁלוֹשׁ לְפָנִים, עֶשְׂרִים וְשֵׁשׁ מֵאָחוֹר.	lahatz haavir tzarikh lihyot esrim veshalosh lefanim esrim veshesh meahor
Check the spare tire, too, please.	תִּבְדוֹק גַּם אֶת הַגַּלְגַּל הָרֶזֶרְבִי, בְּבַקָּשָׁה.	tivdok gam et hagalgal harezervi, bevakasha
Can you mend this puncture (fix this flat)?	תּוּכַל לְתַקֵּן אֶת הַתֶּקֶר הַזֶּה?	tukhal letaken et hateker haze
Will you change this tire, please?	תּוּכַל לְהַחְלִיף אֶת הַגַּלְגַּל הַזֶּה, בְּבַקָּשָׁה?	tukhal lehahlif et hagalgal haze, bevakasha
Will you clean the windshield (windscreen)?	תּוּכַל לְנַקּוֹת אֶת הַשְּׁמָשׁוֹת, בְּבַקָּשָׁה?	tukhal lenakot et hashmashot, bevakasha
Have you a road map of this area?	יֵשׁ לְךָ מַפַּת דְּרָכִים שֶׁל הָאֵזוֹר הַזֶּה?	yesh lekha mapat derakhim shel haezor haze
Where are the toilets?	אֵיפֹה הַשֵּׁרוּתִים?	eyfo hasherutim

Asking the way—Street directions

Excuse me.	סְלִיחָה.	seliha
Can you tell me the way to . . . ?	תּוּכַל לוֹמַר לִי, בְּבַקָּשָׁה, אֵיךְ מַגִּיעִים אֶל . . . ?	tukhal lomar li, bevakasha, ekh magiim el

How do I get to . . . ?	‏אֵיךְ אֲנִי מַגִּיעַ לְ...?‏	ekh ani magia le
Where does this road lead to?	‏לְאָן מוֹבִיל הַכְּבִישׁ הַזֶּה?‏	lean movil hakevish haze
Can you show me where I am on this map?	‏תּוּכַל לְהַרְאוֹת לִי בַּמַּפָּה אֵיפֹה אֲנִי נִמְצָא?‏	tukhal leharot li bamapa eyfo ani nimtza
How far is it to . . . from here?	‏מַה הַמֶּרְחָק מִכָּאן לְ...?‏	ma hamerhak mikan le

Miles into kilometres										
1 mile = 1.609 kilometres (km)										
miles	10	20	30	40	50	60	70	80	90	100
km	16	32	48	64	80	97	113	129	145	161

Kilometres into miles												
1 kilometre (km) = 0.62 miles												
km	10	20	30	40	50	60	70	80	90	100	110	120	130
miles	6	12	19	25	31	37	44	50	56	62	68	75	81

Possible Answers

‏אַתָּה נוֹסֵעַ בַּכְּבִישׁ הַלֹּא־נָכוֹן‏	You're on the wrong road.
‏תַּמְשִׁיךְ יָשָׁר.‏	Go straight ahead.
‏זֶה מִשְּׂמֹאל (מִיָּמִין).‏	It's down there on the left (right).
‏סַע בַּכְּבִישׁ הַהוּא.‏	Go that way.
‏סַע עַד לְצֹמֶת הָרִאשׁוֹן (הַשֵּׁנִי).‏	Go to the first (second) crossroads.
‏תִּפְנֶה שְׂמֹאלָה (יְמִינָה) בָּרַמְזוֹר.‏	Turn left (right) at the traffic lights.

In the rest of this section we'll be more closely concerned with the car itself. We've divided it into two parts:

Part A contains general advice on motoring in Israel. It's essentially for reference, and is therefore to be browsed over, preferably in advance.

Part B is concerned with the practical details of accidents and breakdown. It includes a list of car parts and a list of things that may go wrong with them. All you have to do is to show it to the garage mechanic and get him to point to the items required.

CAR — INFORMATION

Part A

Customs—Documentation

You'll require the following documents:

> passport
> insurance certificate
> registration (log book)
> valid driving licence

Drivers must be in possession of a valid driving licence (in French or English) and a third-party insurance. A valid international permit issued in your country of residence may come in handy. The nationality plate or sticker must be on the car.

Note: The international "green card" isn't valid in Israel. After a three-month stay in the country, tourists are required to pay vehicle licence fees.

Here's my . . .	הִנֵּה הַ . . . שֶׁלִּי.	hine ha . . . sheli
driving licence	רִשְׁיוֹן נְהִיגָה	rishyon nehiga
insurance policy	בִּטּוּחַ	bituah
passport	דַּרְכּוֹן	darkon
I haven't anything to declare.	אֵין לִי מַה לְהַצְהִיר.	en li ma lehatzhir
I've . . .	יֵשׁ לִי . . .	yesh li
a carton of cigarettes	קַרְטוֹן סִיגָרִיּוֹת	karton sigariyot
a bottle of whisky	בַּקְבּוּק וִיסְקִי	bakbuk whisky
a bottle of wine	בַּקְבּוּק יַיִן	bakbuk yayin
We're staying for . . .	אָנוּ נִשְׁאָרִים פֹּה . . .	anu nisharim po
a week	שָׁבוּעַ	shavua
two weeks	שְׁבוּעַיִם	shevuaim
a month	חֹדֶשׁ	hodesh

Roads

Israel is a small country and therefore all places of interest are within very short range. The tourist will find a short but good network of roads. The main highway goes from Tel Aviv to Haifa and is about 60 miles long. The Tel Aviv-Jerusalem road is very scenic, but there are many sharp turns requiring caution.

Although the public transport available has always governed sightseeing, tourists nowadays tend to make their trip more interesting and convenient by bringing a car with them or renting one on the spot.

You'll find that drivers make extensive use of their horns. Don't let this scare you; just be sure to follow the traffic rules.

Speed limits in Israel are as follows:

	Residential areas	Open highways
cars	50 km/h (30 mph)	80/90 km/h (50/56 mph)
motorcycles	40 km/h (25 mph)	70 km/h (44 mph)

Pedestrian crossings are marked by zebra stripes and/or brass studs.

Parking

Use your common sense when parking. The police are normally reasonably lenient with tourists, but don't push your luck too far. You can be fined on the spot for traffic offences.

Park your vehicle in the direction of moving traffic—not against it. Obey the parking regulations which will be indicated by signs.

Excuse me. May I park here?	סְלִיחָה, מוּתָר לְהַחֲנוֹת כָּאן?	seliha, mutar lehahnot kan
How long may I park here?	כַּמָּה זְמַן מוּתָר לַחֲנוֹת כָּאן?	kama zeman mutar lahanot kan
What's the charge for parking here?	כַּמָּה עוֹלָה הַחֲנָיָה?	kama ola hahanaya
Must I leave my lights on?	צָרִיךְ לְהַשְׁאִיר אֶת הָאוֹרוֹת דְּלוּקִים?	tzarikh lehashir et haorot delukim

CAR – INFORMATION

Israeli road signs

Here are some of the main signs and notices you're likely to
encounter when driving in Israel. Obviously, they should be
studied in advance. You can't drive and read at the same
time!

אוֹטוֹסְטְרָדָה	Motorway (expressway)
אֵין כְּנִיסָה	No entry
בְּהַרָצָה	Running-in (car being broken in)
בֵּית חוֹלִים	Hospital
בֵּית סֵפֶר	School
הוֹלְכֵי רֶגֶל	Pedestrians
מַעֲקָף	Diversion (detour)
זְהִירוּת יְלָדִים	Attention, children
זְהִירוּת	Caution
חֲנָיָה	Parking
חֲנָיָה אֲסוּרָה	No parking
כְּבִישׁ בְּתִקּוּן	Road works (men working)
כְּבִישׁ חַד־סִטְרִי	One-way street
כְּבִישׁ חָלָק	Slippery road
כְּבִישׁ צַר	Road narrows
לְאַט	Slow
מַחְסוֹם רַכֶּבֶת	Level-crossing (railroad crossing)
סִבּוּב מְסוּכָּן	Dangerous bend (curve)
סַכָּנָה	Danger
סַע בְּצַד יָמִין	Keep right
סַע לְאַט	Drive slowly
עֲצוֹר	Stop
עֲקִיפָה אֲסוּרָה	No overtaking (no passing)
שֶׁקֶט	Silence

FOR ROAD SIGNS, see also pages 160–161

Part B

Accidents

This section is confined to immediate aid. The legal problems of responsibility and settlement can be taken care of at a later stage.

Your first concern will be for the injured.

Is anyone hurt?	מִישֶׁהוּ נִפְצַע?	mishehu niftza
Don't move.	לֹא לָזוּז.	lo lazuz
It's all right. Don't worry.	הַכֹּל בְּסֵדֶר; אַל תִדְאַג.	hakol beseyder; al tidag
Where's the nearest telephone?	אֵיפֹה הַטֶּלֶפוֹן הַקָּרוֹב בְּיוֹתֵר?	eyfo hatelefon hakarov beyoter
Can I use your telephone? There's been an accident.	אֶפְשָׁר לְהִשְׁתַּמֵשׁ בַּטֶּלֶפוֹן? קָרְתָה תְאוּנָה.	efshar lehishtamesh batelefon? karta teuna
Call a doctor (ambulance) quickly.	קְרָא מַהֵר לְרוֹפֵא (לְאַמְבּוּלַנְס).	kera maher lerofe (leambulans)
There are people injured.	יֵשׁ פְּצוּעִים.	yesh petzuim
Help me get them out of the car.	עֲזוֹר לִי לְהוֹצִיא אוֹתָם מִן הַמְכוֹנִית.	azor li lehotzi otam min hamekhonit

Police—Exchange of information

Please call the police.	קְרָא לַמִּשְׁטָרָה, בְּבַקָּשָׁה.	kera lamishtara, bevakasha
There's been an accident. It's about 2 kilometres from ...	קָרְתָה תְאוּנָה; בְּעֶרֶךְ שְׁנֵי קִילוֹמֶטֶר מִ...	karta teuna; beerekh 2 kilometer mi
I'm on the Haifa— Tel Aviv road, 25 kilometres from Tel Aviv.	אֲנִי בְּכְבִישׁ חַיפָה–תֵל– אָבִיב, עֶשְׂרִים וַחֲמִשָּׁה קִילוֹמֶטֶר מִתֵל–אָבִיב.	ani bakvish Haifa—Tel-Aviv, 25 kilometer miTel-Aviv

CAR – ACCIDENTS

Here's my name and address.	הִנֵּה שְׁמִי וּכְתוֹבְתִּי.	hine shemi ukhtovti
Would you mind acting as a witness?	תַּסְכִּים לְהָעִיד?	taskim lehaid
I'd like an interpreter.	אֲנִי צָרִיךְ מְתוּרְגְּמָן.	ani tzarikh meturgeman

Remember to put out a red triangle warning if the car is out of action or impeding traffic.

Breakdown

. . . and that's what we'll do with this section: break it down into four phases.

1. **On the road**
   You ask where the nearest garage is.
2. **At the garage**
   You tell the mechanic what's wrong.
3. **Finding the trouble**
   He tells you what he thinks is wrong.
4. **Getting it fixed**
   You tell him to fix it and, once that's done, settle the account (or argue about it).

Phase 1—On the road

Where's the nearest garage?	אֵיפֹה הַמּוּסָךְ הַקָּרוֹב בְּיוֹתֵר?	eyfo hamusakh hakarov beyoter
Excuse me. My car has broken down. May I use your phone?	סְלִיחָה, הַמְּכוֹנִית שֶׁלִּי הִתְקַלְקְלָה; אֶפְשָׁר לְהִשְׁתַּמֵּשׁ בַּטֶּלֶפוֹן שֶׁלְּךָ?	seliha, hamekhonit sheli hitkalkela; efshar lehishtamesh batelefon shelkha
What's the telephone number of the nearest garage?	מַהוּ מִסְפַּר הַטֶּלֶפוֹן שֶׁל הַמּוּסָךְ הַקָּרוֹב בְּיוֹתֵר?	mahu mispar hatelefon shel hamusakh hakarov beyoter
I've had a breakdown at . . .	אֲנִי עוֹמֵד בְּ . . .	ani omed be

We're on the motorway Tel Aviv–Jerusalem, about 10 kilometres from Jerusalem.	אֲנִי בְּכְבִישׁ תֵּל־אָבִיב – יְרוּשָׁלַיִם, כְּעֶשְׂרָה קִילוֹמֶטֶר מִירוּשָׁלַיִם.	ani bakvish Tel-Aviv-Yerushalaim, ka 10 kilometer miYerushalaim
Can you send a mechanic?	תּוּכַל לִשְׁלוֹחַ מְכוֹנַאי?	tukhal lishloaḥ mekhonai
Can you send a truck to tow my car?	תּוּכַל לִשְׁלוֹחַ גְרָר?	tukhal lishloaḥ gerar
How long will you be?	כַּמָּה זְמַן זֶה יִקַח לְךָ?	kama zeman ze ikaḥ lekha

Phase 2—At the garage

Can you help me?	תּוּכַל לַעֲזוֹר לִי?	tukhal laazor li
I don't know what's wrong with it.	אֵינֶנִי יוֹדֵעַ מַה הִתְקַלְקֵל.	eyneni yodea ma hitkalkel
I think there's something wrong with the . . .	מַשֶּׁהוּ לֹא בְּסֵדֶר עִם . . .	mashehu lo beseyder im
battery	הַמַּצְבֵּר	hamatzber
brakes	הַבְּלָמִים	habalamim
bulbs	הַמְּנוֹרוֹת	hamenorot
clutch	הַמַּצְמֵד	hamatzmed
cooling system	הַקִירוּר	hakirur
contact	הַהַצָּתָה	hahatzata
dimmers	הָעַמְמוֹר	haamamor
dynamo	הַדִּינָמוֹ	hadinamo
electrical system	מַעֲרֶכֶת הַחַשְׁמָל	maarekhet hahashmal
engine	הַמָּנוֹעַ	hamanoa
gears	הַהִלּוּכִים	hahilukhim
handbrake	בְּלָם הַיָּד	balam hayad
headlight	אוֹרוֹת קִדְמִיִים	orot kidmiim
horn	הַצּוֹפָר	hatzofar
ignition system	מַעֲרֶכֶת הַהַצָּתָה	maarekhet hahatzata
indicator	הַמְהַבְהֵב (הַוִּינְקֶר)	hamehavhev (havinker)

CAR – REPAIRS

lights	הָאוֹרוֹת	haorot
brake light	אוֹר הַבֶּלֶם	or habalam
reversing (back-up) light	אוֹר הַהִילוּךְ הַאֲחוֹרִי	or hahilukh haahori
tail lights	אוֹרוֹת אֲחוֹרִיִים	orot ahoriim
lubrication system	מַעֲרֶכֶת הַסִיכָה	maarekhet hasikha
pedal	הַדַוְשָׁה	hadavsha
reflectors	הַמַחְזִירוֹרִים	hamahzirorim
sparking plugs	הַמַצָתִים	hamatzatim
starting motor	הַהַתְנָעָה	hahatnaa
steering	הַהֶגֶה	hahege
suspension	הַקְפִיצִים	hakefitzim
transmission	הַתִמְסוֹרֶת	hatimsoret
wheels	הַגַלְגַלִים	hagalgalim
wipers	הַמַגָבִים	hamagavim

RIGHT	LEFT		FRONT	BACK
יָמִינָה	שְׂמֹאלָה		קָדִימָה	אֲחוֹרָה
(yamina)	(semola)		(kadima)	(ahora)

It's . . .	זֶה . . .	ze
bad	מְקוּלְקָל	mekulkal
blown	נִשְׂרָף	nisraf
broken	שָׁבוּר	shavur
burnt	שָׂרוּף	saruf
cracked	סָדוּק	saduk
defective	פָּגוּם	pagum
disconnected	מְנוּתָק	menutak
dry	יָבֵשׁ	yavesh
frozen	קָפוּא	kafu
jammed	נִתְפַּס	nitpas
knocking	דוֹפֵק	dofek

leaking	נוֹזֵל	nozel
loose	רוֹפֵף	rofef
misfiring	מִשְׁתָּעֵל	mishtael
noisy	רוֹעֵשׁ	roesh
not working	לֹא פּוֹעֵל	lo poel
overheating	מְחֻמָּם יוֹתֵר מִדַּי	mehamem yoter miday
short-circuiting	קַצֵּר	ketzer
slack	תָּלוּי	taluy
slipping	מַחְלִיק	mahlik
stuck	תָּקוּעַ	takua
vibrating	רוֹעֵד	roed
weak	חַלָּשׁ	halash
worn	שָׁחוּק	shahuk
The car won't start.	אִי־אֶפְשָׁר לְהַתְנִיעַ אֶת הַמְכוֹנִית.	i-efshar leatnia et hamekhonit
It's locked and the keys are inside.	הַמְכוֹנִית נְעוּלָה וְהַמַּפְתְּחוֹת בִּפְנִים.	hamekhonit neula vehamaftehot bifnim
The fan-belt is too slack.	רְצוּעַת הַמְאַוְרֵר רְפוּיָה.	retzuat hameavrer refuya
The radiator is leaking.	הָרַדְיָאטוֹר נוֹזֵל.	haradyator nozel
The idling needs adjusting.	צָרִיךְ לְכַוֵּן אֶת הַקַּרְבּוּרָטוֹר.	tzarikh lekhaven et hakarburator
The clutch engages too quickly.	הַמַּצְמֵד נִתְפָּס יוֹתֵר מִדַּי מַהֵר.	hamatzmed nitpas yoter miday maher
The steering wheel's vibrating.	הַהֶגֶה רוֹעֵד.	hahege roed
The wipers don't work.	הַמַּגְבִים נֶעֱצָרִים.	hamagavim neetzarim
The pneumatic suspension is weak.	הַמַּתְלֶה חַלָּשׁ.	hamatle halash
The pedal needs adjusting.	צָרִיךְ לְכַוֵּן אֶת הַדַּוְשָׁה.	tzarikh lekhaven et hadavsha

Now that you've explained what's wrong, you'll want to know how long it will take to repair it and arrange yourself accordingly.

How long will it take to repair?	כַּמָה זְמָן יִקַח הַתִיקוּן ?	kama zeman ikaḥ hatikun
Suppose I come back in half an hour (tomorrow)?	אֲנִי יָכוֹל לַחֲזוֹר בְּעוֹד חֲצִי שָׁעָה (מָחָר)?	ani yakhol laḥazor beod ḥatzi shaa (maḥar)
Can you give me a lift into town?	תוּכַל לְהָסִיעַ אוֹתִי הָעִירָה?	tukhal lehasia oti haira
Is there a place to stay nearby?	אוּכַל לַחֲכוֹת כָּאן בְּאֵיזֶה מָקוֹם?	ukhal leḥakot kan beeyze makom

Phase 3—Finding the trouble

It's up to the mechanic either to find the trouble or to repair it. All you have to do is hand him the book and point to the text in Hebrew below.

הִסְתַכֵּל, בְּבַקָשָׁה, בָּרְשִׁימָה וְסַמֵן אֶת הַחֵלֶק הַמְקֻלְקָל. אִם הַלָקוֹחַ שֶׁלְךָ רוֹצֶה לָדַעַת פְּרָטִים תִמְצָא אֶת הַמוּנָח הַמַתְאִים בָּרְשִׁימָה שֶׁלְאַחֲרֶיהָ (שָׁבוּר, קָצָר, וכו׳).*

אֶטֶם הָרֹאש	cylinder head gasket
בּוּכְנָה	piston
בֵּית הָאַרְכּוּבָה	crankcase
בְּלוֹק הַמָנוֹעַ	block
בְּלָמִים	brake
גַל	shaft
גַל הָאַרְכּוּבָה	crankshaft
גַל פִּיקוֹת	camshaft

* Please look at the following alphabetical list and point to the defective item. If your customer wants to know exactly what's wrong with it, pick the applicable term from the next list (broken, short-circuited, etc).

גַּלְגַּלִּים	wheels
גֶּנֶרָטוֹר	generator
דַּוְשַׁת הַמַּצְמֵד	clutch pedal
דִּינָמוֹ	dynamo
דִּיסְקַת הַמַּצְמֵד	clutch plate
הֶגֶה	steering
הִלּוּךְ	gear
הַצָּתָה	contact
חִבּוּר	connection
חוּט	cable
חוּטֵי הַמַּצָּתִים	spark plug leads
טַבָּעוֹת	rings
טַבָּעוֹת הַבּוּכְנָה	piston rings
כּוֹשׁ	stems
מְאַוְרֵר	fan
מִבְרָשׁוֹת	brushes
מוֹט הַהֶגֶה	steering column
מַיִם מְזוּקָקִים	battery liquid
מְיַצֵּב	stabilizer
מֶמְבְּרָנָה	diaphragm
מָנוֹעַ	engine
מְנַחַת זַעֲזוּעִים	shock absorber
מֵסַבִּים	bearings
מֵסַבִּים רָאשִׁיִּים	main bearings
מַסְנֵן	filter
מַסְנֵן אֲוִיר	air filter
מַסְנֵן דֶּלֶק	petrol filter
מַסְנֵן שֶׁמֶן	oil filter
מַעֲרֶכֶת הַחַשְׁמַל	electrical system
מַפְלֵג	distributor
מִפְרָק אוּנִיבֶרְסָלִי	universal joint
מַצְבֵּר	battery
מַצְמֵד	clutch

מָצוֹף	float
מַצָּתִים	spark plugs
מִרְוַח הַשַּׁסְתּוֹם	tappets
מַשְׁאָבָה	pump
מַשְׁאֵבַת בֶּנְזִין	petrol pump
מַשְׁאֵבַת דֶּלֶק	fuel pump
מַשְׁאֵבַת מַיִם	water pump
מִתְלֶה	suspension
מִתְלֶה אֲוִיר	pneumatic suspension
מַתְנֵעַ	starter motor
סִיכָה	grease
סְלִיל	ignition coil
סַנְדְּלֵי הַבְּלָמִים	shoes
פְּלָטִינוֹת	points
פַּס שְׁנַיִם	rack and pinion
צִילִינְדֶּר	cylinder
קְפִיץ הַשַּׁסְתּוֹם	valve spring
קְפִיצִים	springs
קַרְבּוּרָטוֹר	carburettor
רֹאשׁ הַצִּילִינְדֶּר	cylinder head
רַדְיָאטוֹר	radiator
רְפִידָה	lining
רְצוּעַת הַמְאַוְרֵר	fan-belt
שְׁנַיִם	teeth
שַׁסְתּוֹם	valve
עֹגֶן	starter armature
תָּאֵי הַמַּצְבֵּר	battery cells
תּוֹף הַבֶּלֶם	brake drum
תֵּיבַת הַהֶגֶה	steering box
תֵּיבַת הַלּוּכִים	gear box
תִּמְסוֹרֶת	transmission
תִּמְסוֹרֶת אוֹטוֹמָטִית	automatic transmission
תֶּרְמוֹסְטָט	thermostat

הָרְשִׁימָה הַזֹּאת מְצַיֶּנֶת מַה הַקִּלְקוּל וּמַה יֵשׁ לַעֲשׂוֹת בַּמְּכוֹנִית. *

אָזֵן	to balance
אָכוּל	corroded
גָּבוֹהַּ	high
דּוֹפֵק	knocking
הַחְלָפָה	to change
חָדָשׁ	to replace
חִזּוּק	to tighten
חַלָּשׁ	weak
יָבֵשׁ	dry
כִּוּוּן	to adjust
לְטֹשׁ	to grind in
מְחֻמָּם יוֹתֵר מִדַּי	overheating
מִלּוּי מַצְבֵּר	to charge
מְלֻכְלָךְ	dirty
מְנֻתָּק	disconnected
מְפֻתָּל	warped
מִתְחַלֵּק	slipping
מִשְׂחָק	play
מִשְׁתָּעֵל	misfiring
נוֹזֵל	leaking
נָמוּךְ	low
נִקּוּי	to clean
נִשְׂרָף	burnt
נִתְפַּס	jammed
סָדוּק	cracked
פָּגוּם	defective
פֵּרוּק	to strip down
קָפוּא	frozen
קֶצֶר חַשְׁמָלִי	short-circuit
רוֹעֵד	vibrating

CAR – REPAIRS

* The following list contains words about what's wrong or what may need to be done with the car.

רוֹפֵף	slack	
רָפוּי	loose	
רִיפּוּף	to loosen	
שָׁבוּר	broken	
שָׁחוּק	worn	
שָׂרוּף	blown	
תָקוּעַ	stuck	
תֶקֶר	puncture	

Is that serious?	זֶה רְצִינִי?	ze retzini
Can you fix it?	תּוּכַל לְתַקֵן אֶת זֶה?	tukhal letaken et ze
Can you do it now?	תּוּכַל לַעֲשׂוֹת אֶת זֶה עַכְשָׁו?	tukhal laasot et ze akhshav
What's it going to cost?	כַּמָה זֶה יַעֲלֶה?	kama ze yaale
Have you the necessary spare parts?	יֵשׁ לְךָ כָּל חֶלְקֵי הַחִלּוּף?	yesh lekha kol helkey hahiluf

What if he says "no"?

Why can't you do it?	לָמָה אֵינְךָ יָכוֹל לַעֲשׂוֹת אֶת זֶה?	lama enkha yakhol laasot et ze
Is it essential to have that part?	הַאִם הַחֵלֶק הַזֶה הֶכְרֵחִי?	haim hahelek haze hekhrehi
How long is it going to take to get the spare parts?	כַּמָה זְמָן יִקַח לְהַשִׂיג אֶת הַחֵלֶק הַזֶה?	kama zeman ikah lehasig et hahelek haze
Where's the nearest garage that can repair it?	אֵיפֹה הַמוּסָךְ הַקָרוֹב בְּיוֹתֵר שֶׁיוּכַל לְתַקֵן אֶת זֶה?	eyfo hamusakh hakarov beyoter sheyukhal letaken et ze
Well, can you fix it so that I can get as far as . . . ?	תּוּכַל לְתַקֵן אֵיכְשֶׁהוּ שֶׁאוּכַל לְהַגִיעַ לְ . . . ?	tukhal letaken ekhshehu sheukhal lehagia le

If you're really stuck, ask if you can leave the car at the garage. Contact an automobile association—or hire another car.

Settling the bill

| Is everything fixed? | הַכֹּל בְּסֵדֶר? | hakol beseyder |
| How much do I owe you? | כַּמָּה אֲנִי חַיָּב לְךָ? | kama ani ḥayav lekha |

The garage then presents you with a bill. If you're satisfied . . .

Will you take a traveller's cheque?	אַתָּה מְקַבֵּל הַמְחָאוֹת נוֹסְעִים?	ata mekabel hamḥaot nosim
Thanks very much for your help.	תּוֹדָה רַבָּה עַל עֶזְרָתְךָ.	toda raba al ezratkha
This is for you.	זֶה בִּשְׁבִילְךָ.	ze bishvilkha

But you may feel that the workmanship is sloppy or that you're paying for work not done. Get the bill itemized. If necessary, get it translated before you pay.

| I'd like to check the bill first. Will you itemize the work done? | אֲנִי רוֹצֶה לִבְדּוֹק אֶת הַחֶשְׁבּוֹן; תּוּכַל לְפָרֵט כָּל פְּרָט? | ani rotze livdok et haheshbon; tukhal lefaret kol perat |

If the garage still won't back down—and you're sure you're right—get the help of a third party.

Some Israeli road signs

No vehicles

No entry
(one way)

No automobiles

No overtaking
(passing)

Speed limit

Priority to
oncoming traffic

No right turn

No U turn

Residential area,
restricted speed

Stop

Hairpin bend
(curve)

Road junction
ahead

Narrow bridge

Caution

Uneven road

Stop sign ahe

Go straight

 Right turn ahead

 Turn right

Pass obstacle
on the left

 Roundabout
(rotary)

 Minimum speed

 Motor vehicles
only

Pedestrians only

 End of
residential area

 One way

 Parking

First-aid station
ahead

 Picnic ground

 Youth hostel

 Maximum speed
on motorway
(expressway)

 End of motorway
(expressway),
reduce speed

Doctor

Frankly, how much use is a phrase book going to be to you in the case of serious injury or illness? The only phrase you need in such an emergency is . . .

Get a doctor—quick!	רוֹפֵא, מַהֵר!	rofe, maher

But there are minor aches and pains, ailments and irritations that can upset the best planned trip. Here we can help you— and, perhaps, the doctor.

Most doctors will speak English well; others will know enough for your needs. But suppose there's something the doctor can't explain because of language difficulties? We've thought of that. As you'll see, this section has been arranged to enable you and the doctor to communicate. From page 165 to 171, you'll find your side of the dialogue on the upper half of each page; the doctor's is on the lower half.

The whole section has been divided into three parts: illness, wounds, nervous tension. Page 171 is concerned with prescriptions and fees.

General

I need a doctor– quickly.	אֲנִי צָרִיךְ רוֹפֵא, דָחוּף.	ani tzarikh rofe, daḥuf
Is there a doctor in the hotel/house?	יֵשׁ רוֹפֵא בַּמָלוֹן / בַּבַּיִת?	yesh rofe bamalon/ babayit
Where's there a doctor who speaks English?	אֵיפֹה יֵשׁ רוֹפֵא שֶׁמְדַבֵּר אַנְגְלִית?	eyfo yesh rofe shemedaber anglit
Where's the doctor's office?	אֵיפֹה חֲדַר הַקַבָּלָה?	eyfo ḥadar hakabala
What are the office hours?	מֵהֶן שְׁעוֹת הַקַבָּלָה?	mahen sheot hakabala

FOR PHARMACY, see page 108

| Could the doctor come and see me here? | הַאִם הָרוֹפֵא יָכוֹל לָבוֹא וְלִבְדוֹק אוֹתִי כָּאן? | haim harofe yakhol lavo velivdok oti kan |
| What time can the doctor come? | בְּאֵיזֶה שָׁעָה יָכוֹל לָבוֹא הָרוֹפֵא? | beeyze shaa yakhol lavo harofe |

Symptoms

Use this section to tell the doctor what's wrong. Basically, what he'll need to know is:

What?	(ache, pain, bruise, etc.)
Where?	(arm, stomach, etc.)
How long?	(have you had the trouble)

Before you visit the doctor find out the answers to these questions by glancing through the pages that follow. In this way, you'll save time.

Parts of the body

ankle	קַרְסוֹל	karsol
appendix	תוֹסֶפְתָן	toseftan
arm	זְרוֹעַ	zeroa
artery	עוֹרֵק	orek
back	גַב	gav
bladder	שַׁלְפּוּחִית הַשֶּׁתֶן	shalpuḥit hasheten
blood	דָם	dam
bone	עֶצֶם	etzem
breast	שַׁד	shad
chest	חָזֶה	ḥaze
collar-bone	עֶצֶם הַבְּרִיחַ	etzem habariaḥ
ear	אוֹזֶן	ozen
elbow	מַרְפֵּק	marpek
eye/eyes	עַיִן / עֵינַיִים	ayin/eynayim
finger	אֶצְבַּע	etzba

DOCTOR

foot	כַּף הָרֶגֶל	kaf haregel
gland	בַּלּוּטָה	baluta
hand	יָד	yad
head	רֹאשׁ	rosh
heart	לֵב	lev
heel	עָקֵב	akev
hip	מֹתֶן	moten
intestines	מֵעִי דַק	mei dak
joint	פֶּרֶק	perek
kidney	כִּלְיָה	kilya
knee	בֶּרֶךְ	berekh
leg	רֶגֶל	regel
liver	כָּבֵד	kaved
lung	רֵאָה	rea
mouth	פֶּה	pe
muscle	שְׁרִיר	sherir
neck	צַוָּאר	tzavar
nerve	עָצָב	atzav
nervous system	מַעֲרֶכֶת הָעֲצַבִּים	maarekhet haatzabim
nose	אַף	af
rib	צֵלָע	tzela
shoulder	כָּתֵף	katef
skin	עוֹר	or
spine	חוּט הַשִּׁדְרָה	hut hashidra
stomach	קֵיבָה	keyva
tendon	גִּיד	gid
throat	גָּרוֹן	garon
toe	בֹּהֶן הָרֶגֶל	bohen haregel
tongue	לָשׁוֹן	lashon
tonsils	שְׁקֵדִים	shekedim
urine	שֶׁתֶן	sheten
vein	וְרִיד	varid
wrist	פֶּרֶק הַיָּד	perek hayad

PATIENT

Part 1—Illness

I'm not feeling well.	אֲנִי לֹא מַרְגִּישׁ טוֹב.	ani lo margish tov
I'm ill.	אֲנִי חוֹלֶה.	ani hole
I've got a pain here.	יֵשׁ לִי כְּאֵבִים כָּאן.	yesh li keevim kan
His/Her . . . hurts.	יֵשׁ לוֹ כְּאֵבִים בְּ . . .	yesh lo keevim ba
I've got a . . .	יֵשׁ לִי . . .	yesh li
headache/backache/ fever/sore throat	כְּאֵב רֹאשׁ / כְּאֵב גַב / חוֹם / כְּאֵב גָרוֹן	keev rosh/keev gav/hom/ keev garon
I'm constipated.	יֵשׁ לִי עֲצִירוּת.	yesh li atzirut
I've been vomiting.	יֵשׁ לִי הֲקָאוֹת.	yesh li hakaot
I feel . . .	אֲנִי מַרְגִּישׁ . . .	ani margish
ill/sick	רַע / חוֹלֶה	ra/hole
nauseated/shivery	בְּחִילָה / צְמַרְמוֹרֶת	behila/tzemarmoret

DOCTOR

DOCTOR

חֵלֶק 1 – מַחֲלוֹת

מַה יֵּשׁ לְךָ?	What's the trouble?
אֵיפֹה כּוֹאֵב לְךָ?	Where does it hurt?
כַּמָּה זְמַן אַתָּה מַרְגִּישׁ אֶת הַכְּאֵב?	How long have you had this pain?
כַּמָּה זְמַן אַתָּה מַרְגִּישׁ כָּכָה?	How long have you been feeling like this?
תַּפְשִׁיל אֶת הַשַּׁרְווּל.	Roll up your sleeve.
תִּתְפַּשֵּׁט עַד לַמּוֹתֶן.	Please undress down to the waist.
תִּפְשׁוֹט בְּבַקָּשָׁה אֶת הַמִּכְנָסַיִם וְאֶת הַתַּחְתּוֹנִים.	Please remove your trousers and underpants.

PATIENT

I/He/She's got (a/an) . . .	יֵשׁ לִי / לוֹ / לָה . . .	yesh li/lo/la
abscess	מֻגְלָה	mugla
asthma	קַצֶּרֶת	katzeret
boil	מֻרְסָה	mursa
chill	הִצְטַנְּנוּת	hitztanenut
cold	נַזֶּלֶת	nazelet
constipation	עֲצִירוּת	atzirut
convulsions	עֲוִית	avit
cramps	הִתְכַּוְּצוּיוֹת	hitkavtzuyot
diarrhoea	שִׁלְשׁוּל	shilshul
fever	חֹם	ḥom
haemorrhoids	טְחוֹרִים	teḥorim
hay fever	קַדַּחַת הַשַּׁחַת	kadaḥat hashaḥat
hernia	שֶׁבֶר	shever

DOCTOR

שְׁכַב פֹּה, בְּבַקָּשָׁה.	Please lie down over here.
פְּתַח אֶת הַפֶּה.	Open your mouth.
תִּנְשׁוֹם עָמוֹק.	Breathe deeply.
תִּשְׁתָּעֵל, בְּבַקָּשָׁה.	Cough, please.
אֶמְדּוֹד לְךָ אֶת הַחֹם.	I'll take your temperature.
אֶמְדּוֹד לְךָ אֶת לַחַץ הַדָּם.	I'm going to take your blood pressure.
אֶתֵּן לְךָ זְרִיקָה.	I'll give you an injection.
תָּבִיא בְּדִיקַת שֶׁתֶן / צוֹאָה.	I want a specimen of your urine/stools.
זוֹ הַפַּעַם הָרִאשׁוֹנָה שֶׁיֵּשׁ לְךָ דָּבָר כָּזֶה?	Is this the first time you've had this?

PATIENT

indigestion	קִלְקוּל קֵיבָה	kilkul keyva
inflammation of . . .	דַּלֶּקֶת...	daleket
influenza	שַׁפַּעַת	shapaat
morning sickness	בְּחִילוֹת	behilot
rheumatism	שִׁגָּרוֹן	shigaron
stiff neck	כְּאֵב בַּצַּוָּאר	keev batzavar
sunburn	כְּוִיּוֹת שֶׁמֶשׁ	keviyot shemesh
sunstroke	מַכַּת שֶׁמֶשׁ	makat shemesh
tonsillitis	דַּלֶּקֶת שְׁקֵדִים	daleket shekedim
ulcer	כִּיב	kiv
whooping cough	שַׁעֶלֶת	shaelet
wound	פֶּצַע	petza
It's nothing serious, I hope?	זֶה לֹא מַשֶּׁהוּ רְצִינִי, אֲנִי מְקַוֶּה?	ze lo mashehu retzini, ani mekave

---

DOCTOR

אֵין מַה לִדְאוֹג.	It's nothing to worry about.
אַתָּה צָרִיךְ לְהִשָּׁאֵר בַּמִּטָּה ...יָמִים.	You must stay in bed for . . . days.
יֵשׁ לְךָ ...	You've got . . .
נַזֶּלֶת דַּלֶּקֶת פְּרָקִים/דַּלֶּקֶת רֵיאוֹת שַׁפַּעַת/הַרְעָלַת קֵיבָה / דַּלֶּקֶת שֶׁל...	a cold/arthritis/pneumonia/ influenza/food poisoning/ an inflammation of. . .
אַתָּה מְעַשֵּׁן / שׁוֹתֶה יוֹתֵר מִדַּי.	You're smoking/drinking too much.
אַתָּה עָיֵף מִדַּי. אַתָּה זָקוּק לִמְנוּחָה.	You're over-tired. You need a rest.
אֲנִי שׁוֹלֵחַ אוֹתְךָ לְרוֹפֵא מֻמְחֶה.	I want you to see a specialist.
אַתָּה צָרִיךְ לָלֶכֶת לְבֵית־חוֹלִים לִבְדִיקָה כְּלָלִית.	I want you to go to hospital for a general check-up.
אֶרְשׁוֹם לְךָ אַנְטִבִּיוֹטִיקָה.	I'll prescribe an antibiotic.

PATIENT

I'm a diabetic.	אֲנִי חוֹלֶה סַכֶּרֶת.	ani ḥole sakeret
I've a cardiac condition.	אֲנִי חוֹלֶה לֵב.	ani ḥole lev
I had a heart attack in . . .	הָיְתָה לִי הַתְקָפַת לֵב בְּ. . .	hayta li hatkafat lev be
I'm allergic to . . .	אֲנִי אַלֶרְגִי לְ. . .	ani alergi le
This is my usual medicine.	זֹאת הִיא הַתְרוּפָה הָרְגִילָה שֶׁלִי.	zot hi haterufa hargila sheli
I need this medicine.	אֲנִי זָקוּק לַתְרוּפָה זֹאת.	ani zakuk literufa zot
I'm expecting a baby.	אֲנִי בְּהֵרָיוֹן.	ani beherayon
Can I travel?	מוּתָר לִי לִנְסוֹעַ?	mutar li linsoa

DOCTOR

אֵיזֶה כַּמוּת אִינְסוּלִין אַתָה לוֹקֵחַ?	What dose of insulin are you taking?
בְּזְרִיקוֹת אוֹ בְּכַדוּרִים?	Injection or oral?
אֵיזֶה טִפּוּל קִבַּלְתָ?	What treatment have you been having?
אֵיזֶה תְרוּפָה אַתָה לוֹקֵחַ?	What medicine have you been taking?
הָיְתָה לְךָ הַתְקָפַת לֵב (קַלָה).	You've had a (slight) heart attack.
כָּאן לֹא מִשְׁתַמְשִׁים בְּ. . .	We don't use . . .
זֶה דוֹמֶה מְאוֹד.	This is very similar.
מָתַי אַתְ צְרִיכָה לָלֶדֶת?	When is the baby due?
אָסוּר לְךָ לִנְסוֹעַ עַד יוֹם. . .	You can't travel until . . .

PATIENT

Part 2—Wounds

Could you have a look at this . . . ?	... אַתָּה יָכוֹל לִבְדוֹק אֶת הַ	ata yakhol livdok et ha
boil	מוּרְסָה	mursa
bruise	מַכָּה	maka
burn	כְּוִיָּה	keviya
cut	חַתָךְ	hatakh
graze	שְׂרִיטָה	serita
insect bite	עֲקִיצַת חָרָק	akitzat harak
rash	פְּרִיחָה	periha
swelling	נְפִיחוּת	nefihut
wound	פֶּצַע	petza
I can't move my . . .	... אֵינֶנִּי יָכוֹל לְהָזִיז	eyneni yakhol lehaziz
It hurts.	אֶת הַ ... זֶה כּוֹאֵב.	et ha . . . ze koev

DOCTOR

DOCTOR

חלק 2 – פצעים

זֶה (אֵין) מ...	It is (not) infected.
אַתָּה צָרִיךְ לַעֲשׂוֹת צִלוּם רֶנְטְגֶן.	I want you to have an X-ray.
זֶה ...	It's . . .
שָׁבוּר	broken
נֶקַע / קֶרַע	dislocated/torn
מָתַחְתָּ שְׁרִיר.	You've pulled a muscle.
אֶתֵּן לְךָ חוֹמֶר מְחַטֵּא.	I'll give you an antiseptic.
זֶה לֹא רְצִינִי.	It's not serious.
אֲנִי צָרִיךְ לִרְאוֹת אוֹתְךָ בְּעוֹד ... יָמִים.	I want you to come and see me in . . . days' time.

PATIENT

Part 3—Nervous tension

I'm in a nervous state.	אֲנִי עַצְבָּנִי.	ani atzbani
I'm feeling depressed.	יֵשׁ לִי דִּכָּאוֹן.	yesh li dikaon
I want some sleeping pills.	אֲנִי רוֹצֶה כַּמָּה כַּדּוּרֵי שֵׁנָה.	ani rotze kama kadurey sheyna
I can't eat/I can't sleep.	אֵינֶנִּי יָכוֹל לֶאֱכוֹל / לִישׁוֹן.	eyneni yakhol leekhol/lishon
I'm having nightmares.	יֵשׁ לִי סִיּוּטֵי לַיְלָה.	yesh li siyutey layla
Can you prescribe a . . . ?	תּוּכַל לִרְשׁוֹם לִי מַשֶּׁהוּ...?	tukhal lirshom li mashehu
sedative/tranquillizer	לְהַרְגָּעָה	lehargaa
anti-depressant	נֶגֶד דִּכָּאוֹן	neged dikaon

DOCTOR

חלק 3 – עצבים

יֵשׁ לְךָ מֶתַח עַצַּבִּים.	You're suffering from nervous tension.
אַתָּה זָקוּק לִמְנוּחָה.	You need a rest.
אֵיזֶה גְּלוּלוֹת אַתָּה לוֹקֵחַ?	What pills have you been taking?
כַּמָּה לְיוֹם?	How many a day?
כַּמָּה זְמַן הִרְגַּשְׁתָּ כָּכָה?	How long have you been feeling like this?
אֶרְשׁוֹם לְךָ גְּלוּלוֹת.	I'll prescribe some pills.
אֶתֵּן לְךָ מַשֶּׁהוּ לְהַרְגָּעָה.	I'll give you a sedative.

PATIENT

Prescriptions and dosage

What kind of medicine is this?	אֵיזֶה מִן תְּרוּפָה זֹאת?	eyze min terufa zot
How many times a day should I take it?	כַּמָה פְּעָמִים בְּיוֹם?	kama peamim beyom
Must I swallow them whole?	צָרִיךְ לִבְלוֹעַ אוֹתָם כְּמוֹ שֶׁהֵם?	tzarikh livloa otam kemo shehem

Fee

How much do I owe you?	כַּמָה אֲנִי חַיָב לְךָ?	kama ani hayav lekha
Do I pay you now or will you send me your bill?	אֲשַׁלֵם עַכְשָׁו, אוֹ תִשְׁלַח לִי חֶשְׁבּוֹן?	ashalem akhshav o tishlah li heshbon
Thanks for your help, doctor.	תוֹדָה שֶׁעָזַרְתָּ לִי, דוֹקְטוֹר.	toda sheazarta li, doktor

DOCTOR

DOCTOR

חלק 4 – תרופות וכמות

קַח... כַּפִּיוֹת כָּל... שָׁעוֹת.	Take . . . teaspoonsful of this medicine every . . . hours.
קַח... טַבְּלֵטִים בְּכוֹס מַיִם.	Take . . . tablets with a glass of water . . .
...פְּעָמִים בְּיוֹם	. . . times a day
לִפְנֵי כָל אֲרוּחָה / אַחֲרֵי כָל אֲרוּחָה	before each meal/after each meal
בַּבֹּקֶר/בַּלַיְלָה	in the mornings/at night

תשלום

מֵאָה/מָאתַיִם לִירוֹת, בְּבַקָשָׁה.	That's IL 100/200, please.
שַׁלֵם עַכְשָׁיו, בְּבַקָשָׁה.	Please pay me now.
אֲשַׁלַח לְךָ חֶשְׁבּוֹן.	I'll send you a bill.

Dentist

Can you recommend a good dentist?	תּוּכַל לְהַמְלִיץ עַל רוֹפֵא שִׁנַּיִם?	tukhal lehamlitz al rofe shinayim
Can I make an appointment to see Dr. . . . ?	מָתַי אוּכַל לִרְאוֹת אֶת דּוֹקְטוֹר . . . ?	matay ukhal lirot et doktor
Can't you possibly make it earlier than that?	אֶפְשָׁר לְהַקְדִּים, בְּבַקָּשָׁה?	efshar lehakdim, bevakasha
I've a toothache.	יֵשׁ לִי כְּאֵב שִׁנַּיִם.	yesh li keev shinayim
I've an abcess.	יֵשׁ לִי מֻגְלָה.	yesh li mugla
This tooth hurts.	הַשֵּׁן כּוֹאֶבֶת לִי.	hashen koevet li
at the top	לְמַעְלָה	lemaala
at the bottom	לְמַטָּה	lemata
in the front	לְפָנִים	lefanim
at the back	בִּפְנִים הַפֶּה	bifnim hape
Can you fix it temporarily?	תּוּכַל לַעֲשׂוֹת תִּקּוּן זְמַנִּי?	tukhal laasot tikun zemani
I don't want it extracted (pulled).	אֵינֶנִּי רוֹצֶה עֲקִירָה.	eyneni rotze akira
I've lost a filling.	נָפְלָה לִי סְתִימָה.	nafla li setima
The gum is very sore/ The gum is bleeding.	הַחֲנִיכַיִם כּוֹאֲבִים לִי מְאֹד / יֵשׁ דִּמּוּם.	hahanikhayim koavim li meod/yesh dimum

Dentures

I've broken this denture.	הַשִּׁנַּיִם הַתּוֹתָבוֹת נִשְׁבְּרוּ לִי.	hashinayim hatotavot nishberu li
Can you repair this denture?	תּוּכַל לְתַקֵּן לִי אֶת הַשִּׁנַּיִם הַתּוֹתָבוֹת?	tukhal letaken li et hashinayim hatotavot
When will it be ready?	מָתַי זֶה יִהְיֶה מוּכָן?	matay ze ihye mukhan

Optician

I've broken my glasses.	נִשְׁבְּרוּ לִי הַמִּשְׁקָפַיִם.	nishberu li hamishkafaim
Can you repair them for me?	תּוּכַל לְתַקֵּן לִי אוֹתָם?	tukhal letaken li otam
When will they be ready?	מָתַי יִהְיוּ מוּכָנִים?	matay ihyu mukhanim
Can you change the lenses?	תּוּכַל לְהַחֲלִיף אֶת הָעֲדָשׁוֹת?	tukhal lehahlif et haadashot
I want some contact lenses.	אֲנִי רוֹצֶה עֲדָשׁוֹת מַגָּע.	ani rotze adashot maga
I want tinted lenses.	אֲנִי רוֹצֶה עֲדָשׁוֹת צִבְעוֹנִיּוֹת.	ani rotze adashot tzivoniyot
I'd like to buy a pair of binoculars.	אֲנִי רוֹצֶה לִקְנוֹת מִשְׁקֶפֶת.	ani rotze liknot mishkefet
How much do I owe you?	כַּמָּה אֲנִי חַיָּב לְךָ?	kama ani hayav lekha
Do I pay you now or will you send me your bill?	צָרִיךְ לְשַׁלֵּם עַכְשָׁו אוֹ תִשְׁלַח לִי חֶשְׁבּוֹן?	tzarikh leshalem akhshav o tishlakh li heshbon

OPTICIAN

FOR NUMBERS, see page 175

Reference section

Countries

At publication date, there were 132 member states in the
United Nations. Here are some of them and a few other
geographical names, too.

Africa	אַפְרִיקָה	Afrika
Asia	אַסְיָה	Asia
Australia	אוֹסְטְרַלְיָה	Ostralia
Canada	קָנָדָה	Kanada
Egypt	מִצְרַיִם	Mitzraim
Europe	אֵירוֹפָּה	Eyropa
France	צָרְפַת	Tzorfat
Germany	גֶרְמַנְיָה	Germania
Great Britain	אַנְגְלִיָה	Anglia
Greece	יָוָן	Yavan
Ireland	אִירְלַנְד	Irland
Italy	אִיטַלְיָה	Italia
Jordan	יַרְדֵן	Yarden
Latin America	אַמֵרִיקָה הַלָטִינִית	Amerika Halatinit
Lebanon	לְבָנוֹן	Levanon
Near East	הַמִזְרָח הַתִיכוֹן	Hamizraḥ Hatikhon
Netherlands	הוֹלַנְד	Holand
New Zealand	נְיוּ-זִילַנְד	New Ziland
North America	צְפוֹן-אַמֵרִיקָה	Tzefon Amerika
South Africa	דְרוֹם אַפְרִיקָה	Derom Afrika
Spain	סְפָרַד	Sefarad
Sweden	שְׁוֵדְיָה	Shvedia
Switzerland	שְׁוַויְיץ	Shvaytz
Syria	סוּרְיָה	Suria
Turkey	תוּרְכִּיָה	Turkia
United States	אַרְצוֹת הַבְּרִית	Artzot-Habrit

Numbers

אֶחָד	1	ehad
שְׁנַיִם	2	shenayim
שְׁלוֹשָׁה	3	shelosha
אַרְבָּעָה	4	arbaa
חֲמִשָּׁה	5	hamisha
שִׁשָּׁה	6	shisha
שִׁבְעָה	7	shiva
שְׁמוֹנָה	8	shemona
תִּשְׁעָה	9	tisha
עֲשָׂרָה	10	asara
אַחַד־עָשָׂר	11	ahad-asar
שְׁנֵים־עָשָׂר	12	sheneym-asar
שְׁלוֹשָׁה־עָשָׂר	13	shelosha-asar
אַרְבָּעָה־עָשָׂר	14	arbaa-asar
חֲמִשָּׁה־עָשָׂר	15	hamisha-asar
שִׁישָׁה־עָשָׂר	16	shisha-asar
שִׁבְעָה־עָשָׂר	17	shiva-asar
שְׁמוֹנָה־עָשָׂר	18	shemona-asar
תִּשְׁעָה־עָשָׂר	19	tisha-asar
עֶשְׂרִים	20	esrim
עֶשְׂרִים וְאֶחָד	21	esrim veehad
עֶשְׂרִים וּשְׁנַיִם	22	esrim ushnayim
עֶשְׂרִים וּשְׁלוֹשָׁה	23	esrim ushlosha
עֶשְׂרִים וְאַרְבָּעָה	24	esrim vearbaa
עֶשְׂרִים וַחֲמִשָּׁה	25	esrim vehamisha
עֶשְׂרִים וְשִׁשָּׁה	26	esrim veshisha
עֶשְׂרִים וְשִׁבְעָה	27	esrim veshiva
עֶשְׂרִים וּשְׁמוֹנָה	28	esrim ushmona
עֶשְׂרִים וְתִשְׁעָה	29	esrim vetisha
שְׁלוֹשִׁים	30	sheloshim
שְׁלוֹשִׁים וְאֶחָד	31	sheloshim veehad

שְׁלוֹשִׁים וּשְׁנַיִם	32	sheloshim ushnayim
אַרְבָּעִים	40	arbaim
חֲמִישִׁים	50	ḥamishim
שִׁישִׁים	60	shishim
שִׁבְעִים	70	shivim
שְׁמוֹנִים	80	shemonim
תִּשְׁעִים	90	tishim
תִּשְׁעִים וְאֶחָד	91	tishim veeḥad
מֵאָה	100	mea
מֵאָה וְאֶחָד	101	mea veeḥad
מֵאָה וַעֲשָׂרָה	110	mea vaasara
מֵאָה וְעֶשְׂרִים	120	mea veesrim
מֵאָה וּשְׁלוֹשִׁים	130	mea ushloshim
מֵאָה וְאַרְבָּעִים	140	mea vearbaim
מֵאָה וַחֲמִישִׁים	150	mea veḥamishim
מֵאָה וְשִׁישִׁים	160	mea veshishim
מֵאָה וְשִׁבְעִים	170	mea veshivim
מֵאָה וּשְׁמוֹנִים	180	mea ushmonim
מֵאָה וְתִשְׁעִים	190	mea vetishim
מָאתַיִם	200	mataim
שְׁלוֹשׁ מֵאוֹת	300	shelosh meot
אַרְבַּע מֵאוֹת	400	arba meot
חֲמֵשׁ מֵאוֹת	500	ḥamesh meot
שֵׁשׁ מֵאוֹת	600	shesh meot
שְׁבַע מֵאוֹת	700	sheva meot
שְׁמוֹנֶה מֵאוֹת	800	shemone meot
תְּשַׁע מֵאוֹת	900	tesha meot
אֶלֶף	1,000	elef
אֶלֶף וּמֵאָה	1,100	elef umea
חֲמֵשֶׁת אֲלָפִים	5,000	ḥameshet alafim
עֲשֶׂרֶת אֲלָפִים	10,000	aseret alafim
מֵאָה אֶלֶף	100,000	mea elef
מִלְיוֹן	1,000,000	milyon

first	רִאשׁוֹן	rishon
second	שֵׁנִי	sheni
third	שְׁלִישִׁי	shelishi
fourth	רְבִיעִי	revii
fifth	חֲמִישִׁי	hamishi
sixth	שִׁשִּׁי	shishi
seventh	שְׁבִיעִי	shevii
eighth	שְׁמִינִי	shemini
ninth	תְּשִׁיעִי	teshii
tenth	עֲשִׂירִי	asiri
once	פַּעַם	paam
twice	פַּעֲמַיִם	paamaim
three times	שָׁלוֹשׁ פְּעָמִים	shalosh peamim
a half	חֲצִי	hatzi
a quarter	רֶבַע	reva
one third	שְׁלִישׁ	shelish
a pair of	זוּג	zug
a dozen	תְּרֵיסָר	tereysar
1973 (year)	שָׁנָה אֶלֶף תְּשַׁע מֵאוֹת שִׁבְעִים וְשָׁלוֹשׁ	shana elef tesha meot shivim veshalosh
1974	אֶלֶף תְּשַׁע מֵאוֹת שִׁבְעִים וְאַרְבַּע	elef tesha meot shivim vearba
1975	אֶלֶף תְּשַׁע מֵאוֹת שִׁבְעִים וְחָמֵשׁ	elef tesha meot shivim vehamesh

The year round . . .

Here are the average temperatures for some cities (in Fahrenheit degrees).

	Jerusalem	Haifa	Tel Aviv	Tiberias	Eilat
Winter	45°–60°	50°–63°	48°–66°	54°–70°	52°–72°
Summer	67°–83°	62°–83°	59°–88°	67°–98°	73°–103°

Time

אַחַת
ahat

חֲמִשָּׁה לִשְׁתַּיִם
hamisha lishtayim

עֲשָׂרָה לִשְׁתַּיִם
asara lishtayim

רֶבַע לִשְׁתַּיִם
reva lishtayim

עֶשְׂרִים לִשְׁתַּיִם
esrim lishtayim

עֶשְׂרִים וַחֲמִשָּׁה לִשְׁתַּיִם
esrim vahamisha lishtayim

אַחַת וָחֵצִי
ahat vahetzi

אַחַת וַחֲמִשָּׁה
ahat vahamisha

אַחַת וַעֲשָׂרָה
ahat vaasara

אַחַת וָרֶבַע
ahat vareva

אַחַת וְעֶשְׂרִים
ahat veesrim

אַחַת עֶשְׂרִים וַחֲמִשָּׁה
ahat esrim vahamisha

Useful expressions

What time is it?	מַה הַשָּׁעָה?	ma hashaa
Excuse me. Can you tell me the time?	סְלִיחָה, מַה הַשָּׁעָה?	seliha, ma hashaa
I'll meet you at . . . tomorrow.	נִפָּגֵשׁ מָחָר בְּשָׁעָה...	nipagesh mahar beshaa
I'm so sorry I'm late.	אֲנִי מִצְטַעֵר עַל הָאִחוּר.	ani mitztaer al haihur
after	אַחֲרֵי	aharey
before	לִפְנֵי	lifney
early	מוּקְדָם	mukdam
in time	בַּזְמַן	bazman
late	מְאוּחָר	meuhar
midnight	חֲצוֹת	hatzot
noon	צָהֳרַיִם	tzohorayim

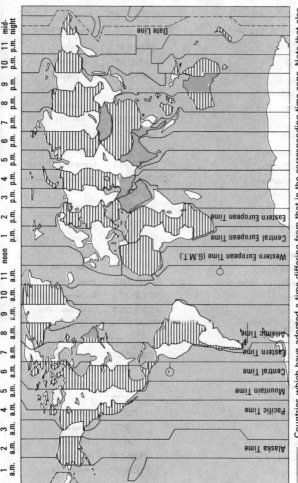

Countries which have adopted a time differing from that in the corresponding time zone. Note that also in the USSR, official time is one hour ahead of the time in each corresponding time zone. In summer, numerous countries advance time one hour ahead of standard time.

Days

What day is it today?	?אֵיזֶה יוֹם הַיּוֹם	eyze yom hayom
Sunday	יוֹם רִאשׁוֹן	yom rishon
Monday	יוֹם שֵׁנִי	yom sheni
Tuesday	יוֹם שְׁלִישִׁי	yom shelishi
Wednesday	יוֹם רְבִיעִי	yom revii
Thursday	יוֹם חֲמִישִׁי	yom hamishi
Friday	יוֹם שִׁשִּׁי	yom shishi
Saturday	שַׁבָּת	shabat
in the morning	בַּבֹּקֶר	baboker
during the day	בְּמֶשֶׁךְ הַיּוֹם	bemeshekh hayom
in the afternoon	אַחַר הַצָּהֳרַיִם	ahar hatzohorayim
in the evening	בָּעֶרֶב	baerev
at night	בַּלַּיְלָה	balayla
yesterday	אֶתְמוֹל	etmol
today	הַיּוֹם	hayom
tomorrow	מָחָר	mahar
two days ago	לִפְנֵי יוֹמַיִם	lifney yomayim
in three days' time	בְּעוֹד שְׁלוֹשָׁה יָמִים	beod shelosha yamim
last week	בְּשָׁבוּעַ שֶׁעָבַר	bashavua sheavar
next week	בְּשָׁבוּעַ הַבָּא	bashavua haba
birthday	יוֹם הֻלֶּדֶת	yom huledet
day	יוֹם	yom
day off	יוֹם חוּפְשָׁה	yom hufsha
holiday	חֹפֶשׁ	hofesh
holidays	חַגִּים	hagim
month	חֹדֶשׁ	hodesh
vacation	חוּפְשָׁה	hufsha
week	שָׁבוּעַ	shavua
weekday	יוֹם חוֹל	yom hol
weekend	סוֹף שָׁבוּעַ	sof shavua
working day	יוֹם עֲבוֹדָה	yom avoda

Months

January	יַנּוּאָר	Yanuar
February	פֶבְּרוּאָר	Februar
March	מֶרְץ	Mertz
April	אַפְּרִיל	April
May	מַאי	May
June	יוּנִי	Yuni
July	יוּלִי	Yuli
August	אוֹגוּסְט	August
September	סֶפְּטֶמְבֶּר	September
October	אוֹקְטוֹבֶּר	Oktober
November	נוֹבֶמְבֶּר	November
December	דֶצֶמְבֶּר	Detzember
since June	מֵאָז יוּנִי	meaz Yuni
during the month of August	בְּמֶשֶׁךְ חֹדֶשׁ אוֹגוּסְט	bemeshekh ḥodesh August
last month	הַחֹדֶשׁ שֶׁעָבַר	hahodesh sheavar
next month	בַּחֹדֶשׁ הַבָּא	bahodesh haba
the month before	לִפְנֵי חֹדֶשׁ	lifney ḥodesh
the next month	בְּעוֹד חֹדֶשׁ	beod ḥodesh
July 1st	הָרִאשׁוֹן בְּיוּלִי	harishon be Yuli
March 17th	הַשִּׁבְעָה־עָשָׂר בְּמֶרְץ	hashiva-asar beMertz

Seasons

spring	אָבִיב	aviv
summer	קַיִץ	kaitz
autumn	סְתָיו	setav
winter	חֹרֶף	horef
in spring	בָּאָבִיב	baaviv
during the summer	בְּמֶשֶׁךְ הַקַּיִץ	bemeshekh hakaitz
in autumn	בַּסְּתָיו	bastav
during the winter	בְּמֶשֶׁךְ הַחֹרֶף	bemeshekh hahoref

Public holidays

Two kinds of calendars are in use in Israel. The Gregorian calendar—which is the one we use—is current in normal daily activities. However, newspapers, radio stations and official documents follow the Hebrew lunar calendar. This calendar starts, according to tradition, with creation. 1973 A.D. would be the year 5733 of the lunar calendar. There are seven leap years in each cycle of 19 years; each leap year has a 13th month of 30 days. Thus, the lunar calendar corresponds to the Gregorian calendar. The lunar year has twelve months of 29 or 30 days:

תִּשְׁרֵי	**Tishrey**	(September–October)
חֶשְׁוָן	**Heshvan**	(October–November)
כִּסְלֵו	**Kislev**	(November–December)
טֵבֵת	**Tevet**	(December–January)
שְׁבָט	**Shevat**	(January–February)
אֲדָר	**Adar**	(February–March)
נִיסָן	**Nisan**	(March–April)
אִיָּר	**Iyar**	(April–May)
סִיוָן	**Sivan**	(May–June)
תַמוּז	**Tamuz**	(June–July)
אָב	**Av**	(July–August)
אֱלוּל	**Elul**	(August–September)

Given below are the most important public holidays.

1st and 2nd Tishrey	Jewish New Year
10th Tishrey	Day of Atonement
15th to 21st Tishrey	Feast of Tabernacles; only the first and last days are holidays, the others semi-holidays.
15th to 21st Nisan	Passover; the feast on the first night is called *seder*; only the first and last days of Passover are holidays; the others are semi-holidays.
5th Iyar	Independence Day
6th Sivan	Pentecost
9th Av	Destruction of the Temple

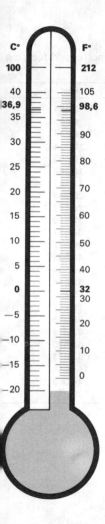

Conversion tables

To change centimetres into inches, multiply by .39.

To change inches into centimetres, multiply by 2.54.

Centimeters and inches

	in.	feet	yards
1 mm	0,039	0,003	0,001
1 cm	0,39	0,03	0,01
1 dm	3,94	0,32	0,10
1 m	39,40	3,28	1,09

	mm	cm	m
1 in.	25,4	2,54	0,025
1 ft.	304,8	30,48	0,304
1 yd.	914,4	91,44	0,914

(32 metres = 35 yards)

Temperature

To convert Centigrade into degrees Fahrenheit, multiply Centigrade by 1.8 and add 32.

To convert degrees Fahrenheit into Centigrade, subtract 32 from Fahrenheit and divide by 1.8.

Metres and feet

The figure in the middle stands for both metres and feet, e.g.
1 metre = 3,281 ft. and 1 foot = 0,30 m.

Metres		Feet
0.30	1	3.281
0.61	2	6.563
0.91	3	9.843
1.22	4	13.124
1.52	5	16.403
1.83	6	19.686
2.13	7	22.967
2.44	8	26.248
2.74	9	29.529
3.05	10	32.810
3.35	11	36.091
3.66	12	39.372
3.96	13	42.635
4.27	14	45.934
4.57	15	49.215
4.88	16	52.496
5.18	17	55.777
5.49	18	59.058
5.79	19	62.339
6.10	20	65.620
7.62	25	82.023
15.24	50	164.046
22.86	75	246.069
30.48	100	328.092

Other conversion charts

REFERENCE SECTION

Weight conversion

The figure in the middle stands for both kilograms and pounds, e.g., 1 kilogram = 2.205 1b. and 1 pound = 0.45 kilograms.

Kilograms (kg.)		Avoirdupois pounds
0.45	1	2.205
0.90	2	4.405
1.35	3	6.614
1.80	4	8.818
2.25	5	11.023
2.70	6	13.227
3.15	7	15.432
3.60	8	17.636
4.05	9	19.840
4.50	10	22.045
6.75	15	33.068
9.00	20	44.889
11.25	25	55.113
22.50	50	110.225
33.75	75	165.338
45.00	100	220.450

צָפוֹן
(tzafon)
NORTH

מַעֲרָב
(maarav)
WEST

מִזְרָח
(mizrah)
EAST

SOUTH
(darom)
דָּרוֹם

What does that sign mean?

You're sure to find some of these signs and notices on your trip.

אָזַל	Sold out
אֵין כְּנִיסָה	No entrance
אֵין מַעֲבָר	No trespassing
אָסוּר ...	. . . forbidden
אָסוּר לָגַעַת	Don't touch
אָסוּר לְעַשֵּׁן	No smoking
גְּבָרוֹת / נָשִׁים	Ladies
גְּבָרִים	Gentlemen
דְּחוֹף	Push
דֶּרֶךְ פְּרָטִית / שְׁבִיל פְּרָטִי	Private road
זְהִירוּת	Caution
זְהִירוּת – כֶּלֶב נוֹשֵׁךְ	Beware of the dog
יְצִיאָה	Exit
יְצִיאַת חֵרוּם	Emergency exit
כְּנִיסָה	Entrance
כְּנִיסָה חָפְשִׁית	Free entrance
לְהַשְׂכָּרָה	For hire
לִמְכִירָה	For sale
מוֹדִיעִין	Information
מַעֲלִית	Lift (elevator)
מְשׁוֹךְ	Pull
נָא לְצַלְצֵל	Please ring
סָגוּר	Closed
סַכָּנָה	Danger
סַכָּנַת מָוֶת	Mortal danger
פָּנוּי	Vacant
פְּרָטִי	Private
קוּפָּה	Cashier
תָּפוּס	Occupied

REFERENCE SECTION

Emergency!

By the time the emergency is upon you, it's too late to turn
to this page to find the Hebrew for "Stop or I'll scream!"
So have a look at this short list beforehand—and, if you want
to be on the safe side, learn the expressions shown in capitals.

Be quick	תִּזְדָּרֵז	tizdarez
Call the police	קְרָא לַמִּשְׁטָרָה	kera lamishtara
CAREFUL	תִּזָּהֵר	tizaher
Come here	בֹּא הֵנָּה	bo hena
Come in	יָבוֹא	yavo
Fire	אֵשׁ	esh
Gas	גַז	gaz
Get a doctor	קְרָא לְרוֹפֵא	kera lerofe
Get help quickly	קְרָא לְעֶזְרָה, מַהֵר	kera leezra, maher
Go away	תִּסְתַּלֵּק	tistalek
HELP	הַצִּילוּ	hatzilu
I'm ill	אֲנִי חוֹלֶה	ani hole
I'm lost	תָּעִיתִי בַּדֶּרֶךְ	taiti baderekh
Leave me alone	עֲזוֹב אוֹתִי	azov oti
Lie down	שְׁכַב	shekhav
Listen	שְׁמַע־נָא	shema-na
Look	תִּסְתַּכֵּל	tistakel
LOOK OUT	שִׂים לֵב	sim lev
POLICE	מִשְׁטָרָה	mishtara
Quick	מַהֵר	maher
STOP	עֲצוֹר	atzor
Stop here	עֲצוֹר כָּאן	atzor kan
Stop that man	עֲצוֹר אֶת הָאִישׁ הַזֶּה	atzor at haish haze
STOP THIEF	תְּפוֹס אֶת הַגַּנָּב	tefos et haganav
Stop or I'll scream	תַּפְסִיק מִיָּד	tafsik miyad

REFERENCE SECTION

FOR CAR ACCIDENTS, see page 149

Some Arabic expressions

Excuse me.	عدم مؤاخذه	adam muakhaze
Hello.	مرحبا	marḥaba
Good-bye.	الله معك	allah maak
Yes/No.	نعم / لا	naam/la
Please.	لطفاً	lutfan
Thank you.	شكراً	shukran
Waiter, please.	اسمع يا	ismaya
I'd like . . .	بدّي	biddi
Where are the toilets?	فين المراحيض	fen elmaraḥid
How much is that?	هذا بكم	hada bikam
Could you tell me . . . ?	قول لي	ull li
where/when/why	فين / متى / ليش	fen/mata/lesh
Help me, please.	ساعدني	saedni
What time is it?	ايه الوقت	eh elwakt
one/first	واحد / اول	waḥed/awwal
two/second	اثنين / الثاني	itnen/itani
three/third	ثلاثة / الثالث	talata/italet
What does this mean?	شو معنه هذه	shu maanah had
Do you speak English?	بتكلم انجليزي	btitkallem inglizi
Show me . . .	ورني	warini
I'll give you . . . for it.	بدفع فيها	bidfa fiha
That's too much.	غالي	rhali

Where can I find a . . . ?	فين بلاقي	fen belaki
taxi/bus	تكسي / باص	taxi/bus
Is this hand-made?	هذا صنع يد	hada suna yad
Is it made of . . . ?	مصنوع من . . .	masnu min . . .
gold/silver	ذهب / فضه	dahab/fidah
brass/copper	نحاس	nhas
cotton/wool	قطن / صوف	kutun/suf
genuine leather	جلد اصلي	djild asli
red/green	احمر / اخضر	ahmar/akhdar
brown/yellow	بني / اصفر	bunni/asfar
blue/black	ازرق / اسود	azrak/asuad
white/orange	ابيض / بردجاني	abyad/burdukani
Where's the . . . street?	فين شارع . . .	fen sharea
Where's the market?	فين سوق	fen suk
Call the police.	اطلب الشرطه	utlub eshortah
Get a doctor/ambulance.	جيب لي طبيب / اسعاف	djib li tabib/isaf
Go away.	امشي	imshi
I'm lost.	ضيعت طريقي	dayyat tariki
I've lost my . . .	ضيعت . . .	dayyat
Look.	شوف	shuf
Quick.	بسرعة	bisurah
Stop thief!	وقف حرامي	wakef harami
Where can I get something to eat/to drink?	فين بقدر آكل / اشرب	fen bakdar akol/ashrab

Index

Quick reference page

Please.	בְּבַקָשָׁה.	bevakasha
Thank you.	תּוֹדָה.	toda
Yes/No.	כֵּן / לֹא.	ken/lo
Excuse me.	סְלִיחָה.	seliha
Waiter, please.	מֶלְצַר!	meltzar
How much is that?	כַּמָה זֶה עוֹלֶה?	kama ze ole
Where are the toilets?	אֵיפֹה הַשֵׁרוּתִים?	eyfo hasherutim

שֵׁרוּתִים	(sherutim)	Toilets
נָשִׁים (nashim)		גְבָרִים (gevarim)

Could you tell me ...?	תּוּכַל לוֹמַר לִי...?	tukhal lomar li
where/when/why	אֵיפֹה / מָתַי / לָמָה	eyfo/matay/lama
Help me, please.	עֲזוֹר לִי, בְּבַקָשָׁה.	azor li, bevakasha
What time is it?	מַה הַשָׁעָה?	ma hashaa
one/first	אֶחָד / רִאשׁוֹן	ehad/rishon
two/second	שְׁנַיִם / שֵׁנִי	shenayim/sheni
three/third	שְׁלוֹשָׁה / שְׁלִישִׁי	shelosha/shelishi
What does this mean?	מַה הָעִנְיָן?	ma hainyan?
I don't understand.	אֵינֶנִי מֵבִין.	eyneni mevin
Just a minute. I'll point out the word.	רֶגַע אֶחָד, אַצְבִּיעַ עַל הַמִלָה.	rega ehad, atzbia al hamila
Do you speak English?	אַתָה מְדַבֵּר אַנְגְלִית?	ata medaber anglit